WRITING RESEARCH PROJECTS *Activities Kit*

Mary Ellen Ledbetter

THE CENTER FOR APPLIED RESEARCH IN EDUCATION
West Nyack, New York 10994

Ledbetter, Mary Ellen.
Writing research projects activities kit : ready-to-use lessons & activities to build research & writing skills for grades 7–12 / Mary Ellen Ledbetter.
p. cm.
Includes bibliographical references and index.
ISBN 0–13–022816–8
1. English language—Composition and exercises—Study and teaching (Secondary) 2. Research—Methodology—Study and teaching (Secondary) 3. Report writing—Study and teaching (Secondary)
I. Title.
LB1631.L338 1998
808'.02—dc21
99–39211
CIP

Printed in the United States of America

10 9 8 7 6 5 4 3 2 1

ISBN 0-13-022816-8

THE CENTER FOR APPLIED RESEARCH IN EDUCATION
West Nyack, NY 10994

On the World Wide Web at http://www.phdirect.com

Dedication

For my mother and father, who introduced me to the world of words, and to my husband, who did his work and mine, so that I could have the time to write.

ABOUT THE AUTHOR

Mary Ellen Ledbetter was born in Texas City, Texas, attended Texas Lutheran College, and graduated from Western Michigan University with a B.A. in English and Speech and from Michigan State University with a Master's degree in English. She has taught in public schools in Michigan and Texas as well as at San Jacinto College in Pasadena, Texas. Ms. Ledbetter has been an instructor in the Writing Process Workshop for teachers, a presenter at TMSA and NCTE, has received Goose Creek CISD's Board of Trustees' Bell Award for Outstanding Teacher in 1995 and 1997, and is currently a presenter/consultant for the Bureau of Education and Research, Bellevue, Washington. Her resource, *Writing Portfolio Activities Kit*, was published by the Center in 1998.

Acknowledgments

The author thanks Bonner Jones--a friend, a brilliant attorney, and a computer whiz--for his patience and time in "unsticking" me when I was stuck. And to his wife Erin for her expertise in reading, revising, and advising--a true friend indeed. Another thanks to Ron Ferris, who helped me cross some rocky computer terrain. Finally, to my aunt and uncle--Earleen and Bill Fuhrhop--who gave me the very generous Christmas present of a new computer and scanner--now I can really fly!

The author also would like to thank her student writers who have shared their work so that maybe others will read and say "Ah, yes..." or "Me, too," or "I see what you mean." They have understood the beauty and the power of language and have never ceased to amaze.

About This Resource

Writing Research Projects Activities Kit provides ready-to-use assignments for library activities that can be done both in and out of the classroom. Specially designed teacher pages give instructions, suggestions, and variations for projects ranging from literary analysis tests to sample research papers in every mode to library book journals and vocabulary projects that can apply not only to the language arts classroom but to other disciplines as well.

Part One, "Library Projects," includes assignments designed to be completed in the classroom and/or as homework with minimal actual library time. These projects are not meant to replace the research paper; rather they provide students with the opportunity to familiarize themselves with various aspects of research (e.g., use of internal documentation, incorporation of quoted textual material into the student's own words, etc.)

Students will learn:

- How to identify literary elements in a work and how to document their inclusion in an assignment based on the student's independent library reading
- How to write book reviews and letters to authors
- How to determine significant points of plot (i.e., rising actions, climax, falling actions) of a novel, explain the action from a character's point of view, and document facts taken from the text--all in a fun "Dear Diary" assignment
- How to interact with their classmates in such projects as "Stump the Reader" and "Circle Response Groups"
- How to write note and bibliographic cards
- How to combine vocabulary usage, research, and letter/post card writing

- How to make bookmarks that will "advertise" their library books
- How to give the dominant impression of a book's protagonist, antagonist, and chosen minor character and support these traits by citing evidence from the text using all methods of characterization
- How to make a brochure that "sells" vocabulary words from their library books or in-class novels by using all modes of writing (i.e., persuasive, comparison/contrast, narrative, how-to, description)
- How to personalize and personify vocabulary words in creative assignments that emphasize techniques of elaboration and stylistic devices in writing

Also included in this section are sample student products **for assignments,** three generic quizzes **on research techniques, a** "Survival Dictionary" **assignment, and a** handy chart **for students to record books read during the semester.**

Part Two, "Narrative Research," introduces an interesting new approach to writing a research paper. After having been presented with models **such as Maureen Daly's "Sixteen," students are given a chance to** analyze the narratives **not only in terms of their literary elements but in their researched facts as well and supplied with** syllabuses, rubrics, and final check sheets **to guide them in the process of writing their own research narratives.**

This section also includes a myriad of activities such as:

- Two variations of narrative research syllabuses
- Five student-interactive rubrics, including such aspects as the inclusion of required literary elements, correct note card form, appropriate footnote usage, and accurate bibliographic entries

About This Resource

- Award-winning student and teacher models
- Class/peer group response sheets
- A library book narrative vignette test and short story research test

Part Three, "Persuasive Research," gives students the opportunity to role play **in the assignment "You Are the Author," to** experiment with persuasion in another genre **in the assignment "Library Book Test--Poem Form," and to** experience the unique concept of using narrative scenario introductions and conclusions **as attention-getters to more traditional persuasive research papers.**

Teachers have at their fingertips:

- Syllabuses for argumentative/persuasive research papers
- Student samples, complete with narrative scenario introductions and conclusions, three body aspects containing internal footnotes, and bibliographic information
- Partner checks and conferences to encourage deep revisionary strategies as well as proofreading techniques
- Reader response sheets for assessing final products
- Review for persuasive research final exam
- Sample final exam for the persuasive mode
- An independent reading assignment requiring persuasive support

Part IV, "Comparison/Contrast Research," reinforces classroom classificatory writing, **adding another dimension of research in the same mode.**

Students will practice:

- Being illustrator and author in a comparison/contrast mode on a test over their independent reading project
- Writing classificatory papers elaborated by researched facts
- Revising their comparison/contrast research papers according to student-interactive rubrics

Part V, "Descriptive Research," includes a library book test **in the descriptive mode, student and teacher** models of descriptive research papers, **as well as** rubrics, response group sheets, and final check sheets.

This unit includes such ideas as:

- Student samples of "Smiley-Face Tricks," which provide student writers with award-winning examples of figurative language, full-circle endings, specific details for effect, and other "tricks" of successful writers
- Student sample of "Methods of Elaboration" required on state-mandated writing tests
- An analysis of a student work designed to highlight techniques that can be used to produce a quality paper in this mode
- Elaboration in the form of researched facts

Part VI, "How-To (Process) Research" **is an opportunity for students to** practice writing across the curriculum **with such sample how-to (process) research papers as "How To Be a Heart"** (science), **"How To Be a Perfect 1950's Housewife"** (history), **and "The Business of Writing"** (language arts).

Also included in this section are

- A "You Are the Teacher" assignment
- A myriad of ideas and topics for writing creative how-to research papers
- Rubrics and final check sheets
- Student response sheets

Part VII, "Internet Research," **helps** familiarize students with Internet capabilities. **Activities are ones that are** relevant **to real life and** fun **for students to explore.**

Students will be able to

- Plan the perfect vacation, complete with taking notes on specific accommodations, famous sights and fun activities, as well as documenting two other aspects of vacationing (e.g., money exchange rate, climate, languages, etc.).
- Plan the perfect date, including restaurants, entertainment, and gifts
- Make a connection between some aspect of their library/in-class novel and a poem

- Understand how allusions add to a literary work
- Practice locating quotations that complement the rising actions, climax, and falling actions of their library book

Using **Writing Research Projects Activities Kit,** students will be taken step-by-step through the process of writing research papers in all modes, will be given award-winning student and teacher models to study, and will be able to choose among a variety of in-class library projects that can be done on a biweekly basis, rather than only during the usual once-a-year assigned library time.

Writing Research Projects Activities Kit provides built-in lesson plans in the form of syllabuses, rubrics, and tests for students and offers options in research that are sure to interest students of all ages.

Mary Ellen Ledbetter

Table of Contents

PART I: LIBRARY PROJECTS / 1

PART III: PERSUASIVE RESEARCH / 163

PART IV: COMPARISON/CONTRAST RESEARCH / 231

PART VII: INTERNET RESEARCH / 361

PART I

LIBRARY PROJECTS

How to Use the Library Book Journal

1. Use the **Library Book Journal** for in-class or out-of-class reading.

2. Students may be **assigned** a certain **literary/reading skill** to cite and explain, or they may **choose** their own skills as they read.

3. **Pages** may be teacher-assigned for **homework** (e.g., 50 pages of homework reading)...

   Or used to test **in-class reading** (e.g., 20 minutes to read in class, which would result in different pages read for each student).

Name:______________________ Class:______________ Date:__________

Library Book Journal

Name of Book:______________________________________

Author:______________________________________

Type of Book:______________________________________

Assessment#________

Date:______________________

Pages Included:______________ **to**______________________

Skill:______________________________________

Assessment Including Specific Examples:

____

____

____

____

____

Assessment #________

Date:______________________

Pages Included:______________ **to**______________________

Skill:______________________________________

Assessment Including Specific Examples:

____

____

____

____

____

Assessment #________________

Date:________________________

Pages Included:________________ **to**________________________________

Skill:____

Assessment Including Specific Examples:

____
____
____
____
____

Assessment #________________

Date:________________________

Pages Included:________________ **to**________________________________

Skill:____

Assessment Including Specific Examples:

____
____
____
____
____

Assessment #________________

Date:________________________

Pages Included:________________ **to**________________________________

Skill:____

Assessment Including Specific Examples:

____
____
____
____

Using the Independent Reading: Literature Terms Assignment

1. Students may be assigned the **Independent Reading: Literature Terms** sheet as they begin their outside-of-class reading project. Terms may be **teacher-assigned** or **student-chosen.** Explanations should show how the term relates to the story as a whole.

2. The **Independent Reading** sheet may be used as an **open-book, in-class "quiz,"** proving the students' familiarity with teacher-chosen concepts and with the content of their novel.

Name:________________ Class:________________ Date:________________

Independent Reading: Literature Terms

Bibliographic Entry for Library Book:______________________________

____

1. **Term:**______________________________

   A. **Quote** (and page #):______________________________

   ____

   ____

   B. **Explanation** as to how this terms **relates to the plot** of the story so far:

   ____

   ____

   ____

2. **Term:**______________________________

   A. **Quote (and page #):**______________________________

   ____

B. Explanation:________________________________

____

____

3. Term:____________________

A. Quote (and page #):__________________________

____

____

B. Explanation:________________________________

____

____

4. Term:____________________

A. Quote (and page #):__________________________

____

____

B. Explanation:________________________________

____

____

5. **Term:** ______________________________

A. Quote (and page #): ______________________________

____

____

B. Explanation: ______________________________

____

____

Extra Credit:

Term: ______________________________

A. Quote (and page #): ______________________________

____

____

B. Explanation: ______________________________

____

How to Use Stump the Reader

1. You may choose to use **Stump the Reader** as a "test" or "class discussion" grade for a class-assigned novel; therefore, each student will be asked a question regarding the same book, of which the entire class will have a background knowledge.

2. Or **Stump the Reader** may be assigned as a "library project," each student being responsible for trying to choose a book to interest the class. As students are asked a question regarding their book, their answers will create interest in their book and serve to provide a "student-approved" reading list.

3. **Stump the Reader** may also be used for books on a teacher-generated list, each student signing up for a certain book.

4. One of the special benefits of **Stump the Reader** is that students are asked to cite only those incidents/examples that answer the questions rather than launching off into a "general" review or summary. The class can monitor answers that stray from the subject, thus giving the entire class practice in various methods of support/elaboration.

Name:______________________________Class:______________Date:_________

Stump the Reader

Assignment:

A. As you read your novel, compose five generic questions that could be applied to any work of fiction and answer the questions in terms of your own book.

☞ You will be graded on the creativity of your questions and the thoroughness of your answers.

☞ Remember to give three examples per question and to include quoted material from the text for at least one example per question.

B. On "Stump the Reader" day, classroom chairs will be moved into a Socratic Debate configuration. Students will ask one of their questions to a member of another team, who must a n s w e r regarding his/her library book. The reader's answer must be thorough enough to prove that he/she has read the book.

1.
Question:______________________________

____

____

Answer:______________________________

____

____

____

____

____

2. Question:______________________________

____

Answer:______________________________

____

____

____

____

____

3. Question:______________________________

____

Answer:______________________________

____

____

____

____

____

____

4. Question:______________________________

____

Answer:______________________________

____

____

____

____

5. Question:

Answer:

Bonus Question:

Answer:

How to Use the Dear Diary Assignment

CONFIDENTIAL

1. **The Dear Diary Assignment** reviews students on the concepts of protagonists versus antagonists, as students are asked to **role play**, assuming the identity of the protagonist of their **library (or in-class) book.**

2. Also, students are required not only to **sequence events** in terms of rising actions, climax, and falling action but to choose which six (minimum) incidents will **best represent the book in its entirety**, giving the reader a clear picture of the action as a whole.

3. Finally, students are given an opportunity to practice **responding in their own words** to material quoted from the text, stressing their points using various methods of elaboration. (See Methods of Elaboration.)

4. Following the assignment are several single entries from student works to serve as **examples** as well as a **"Dear Diary Grammar Mistakes" sheet** that can serve as a **grammatical review** for students.

Name:____________________Class:____________________Date:______________

Dear Diary

Assignment:

1. You will pretend to be the protagonist of your library book. As the action unfolds, you will keep a diary/journal and react to your situation.

2. Each diary/journal entry will begin with a quotation from the book, documented with an internal footnote.

3. Your reaction will be to that quotation, explaining how the situation is affecting you, what you would like to change, etc. Be sure that you explain all the characters, events, etc, in your life so that your entries are clear. Each entry will be 100 words minimum.

4. You will have a minimum of four entries involving rising actions, one entry reacting to the climax of the novel, and one regarding a falling action.

5. Each entry will be illustrated in some way to depict the action/event about which you are writing.

6. Your rubric will be as follows:

   A. Writing that elaborates on your points-- (Use your Smiley-Face Passages and your Elaboration Rubric.)

   B. Grammatical concerns--(Check for spelling, run-ons, fragments, etc.)

Due date:____________________ Bibliographic Entry:____________

Parent signature:__________________ Point Value:__________________

Beth Burnham
Dear Diary Entry

Plague

"Four weeks completely shut away from the rest of humanity. Living on orange juice and apples...no newspapers, no television, no radio, no mail. Isolated" (1).

Dear Diary,

My God, I can't believe the stress I've been through--four long weeks of no news, no family, no friends. I've had to deal with the mosquito bites, the fact that I knew nothing of the world beyond these walls of pain and suffering called the forest. My dad was the only one who supported me, telling me not to worry about the trip, that it would be an experience I would never forget. Boy, was he ever right!

My best friend, Harry (her friends and family call her Harry, but her real name is Harriet), and I actually found a way that some good could come out of this trip: being in the wilderness for such a long time would really slim down my overweight body. Eating lentils and beans and potatoes and drinking oranges and eating apples are really all the kinds of food I need to be eating instead of pigging out on junk food with Harry, whom I can't stand because she is so skinny. Having to look for any other food that I want to eat has made me realize how lazy I am. I will definitely not be spending my days crawling though the woods, looking for insect-infested rotten fruit and berries. Harry and I agree with what my dad had said, "This trip will be a factual learning experience for you."

But we both agree that other than the fact that I will be spending time outside with the buzzing bees, the howling wolves, and the constant awareness that someone is watching me, I will strengthen my mind and senses and come back as a new person.

Nikki Thompson
Dear Diary Entry

The Road to Memphis

"The car, wine-colored and with chrome shimmering in the October sun, came full speed up the road. It was Stacey" (18).

Dear Diary,

Today Stacey, my brother who is twenty, came home from Jackson because he was off work from the box factory. I was kind of angry because we had been waiting for him to come on the bus, that was always late, forever, and then he shows up after the bus had arrived in a '38 Ford. I guess my feelings passed when I saw Stacey. He's almost six feet tall and is very handsome. (Sometimes, I, at seventeen, get a little jealous.) Anyway, I was so happy to see him. I was going back with him to Jackson to go to school on Saturday since I had missed from being sick. What was most exciting was the fact that he bought a car! Boy, was it fine car too! It purred--no roared like a lion--and shone like the Mississippi River in summer!

Billions of questions were racing through my mind. How did he get the money? Where did he buy it? When did he buy it? Why? Who? I finally sorted them all out and discovered that the car was Mr. Jamison's, a friendly man's wife's car. Stacey had put down money on it and was going to pay the rest before the end of the year. Wow! It's a fine new car!

**S.Y.N.T.
e a e i
e   x m
    t e**

Cassie Logan

Name:________________ Class:________________ Date:________________

Dear Diary Grammar Mistakes

The following sentences appeared in students' **"Dear Diary"** assignments. As a grammar review, state the **type of error** in the margin and **correct the mistake(s)** within the sentence.

________________ 1. Four long weeks of no news, no family, no friends.

________________ 2. There is a very deep friendship between Stacey, Christopher-John, Little Man, and me, and me and Jeremy don't think race will ever be able to brake it.

________________ 3. "Cassie I want you to think on gettin' married. I love you Cassie."

________________ 4. There's also other questions.

________________ 5. I broke into the locked box of my Dad, Philip.

________________ 6. Not only do I climb canyons and hike mountains, I also ride my bike as much as possible, I want to be as fit as Wolf.

________________ 7. I just thought about the good times in Atlantic City and the good times between Hugh and I and the good times between Daddy and I.

________________ 8. I wanted Daddy with me so bad to celebrate.

________________ 9. Hope your sitting down because this bit of news is really a shocker.

Dear Diary Grammar Mistakes

_________________ 10. My Aunt Gertrude who lives with us took the call.

_________________ 11. I can't help that I only want what's best for my mother, she deserves someone that meets her standards, and can fulfill all her needs.

_________________ 12. The respected father, the honest, beautiful mother, the daughter that's always so cheerful, and the playful, loving kid brother.

_________________ 13. We never would of made it this far.

_________________ 14. Like always, Cassidy my best friend and I were walking down State Street, and we had a box of pizza because we were heading back to eat some grub.

_________________ 15. I wanted the real truth.

_________________ 16. Maybe because there aren't any reasonable guys around here.

_________________ 17. As the sun peeked out from behind the grey clouds they shot off in a flock.

_________________ 18. Finally we made it to the Rystorms where I bought my aunt a beautiful silver bracelet.

_________________ 19. Jimmy got an audition for Oklahoma.

_________________ 20. "He said, "You're my rabbit's foot, my four-leaf clover."

_________________ 21. She ran away quickly and disappeared into the hedges that separates grumpy old Mrs. Cooper's house and mine.

_________________ 22. I think the Russell's will be kind to us.

_________________ 23. I wish Jessie, my best friend, lived closer so she could ride the bus with me, and I wouldn't be nervous. When the bus arrived at school, I rushed into the crowd, and that's when Jessie called out my name.

_________________ 24. Mike then replied, "they took a sentimental journey to the center of the earth."

_________________ 25. While I was waiting I wished to turn twenty-one and catch that whale.

Answers to:

Dear Diary Grammar Mistakes

1. **Fragment:** Four...have been depressing.
2. **Preposition Usage:** among
   Courtesy Pronoun Rule: Jeremy and I
   Spelling: break
3. **Comma Usage (Direct Address):** Cassie,....you, Cassie
4. **Subject/Verb Agreement:** There are
5. **Capitalization (Family Relationships):** dad
6. **Run-On:** possible.
7. **Pronoun Case (Object of a Preposition):** between Hugh and me; between Daddy and me
8. **Adverb Usage:** badly
9. **Spelling:** you're
10. **Comma Usage (Non-Restrictive Clause):** Gertrude,...us,
11. **Run-On:** mother.
    Incorrect Use of Comma (No Comma between Compound Verbs) : standards and can
12. **Fragment:** I loved reading about....
13. **Preposition Substituting for Helping Verb:** would have made
14. **Comma Usage (Appositive):** Cassidy,...friend,
15. **Redundancy:** I wanted the truth.
16. **Fragment:** Maybe there aren't....
17. **Comma Usage (Introductory Adverb Clause):** clouds,
18. **Comma Usage (Non-Restrictive Clause):** Rystorms
19. **Underlining (Plays/Musicals):** Oklahoma
20. **Quotation Usage:** He said, "You're ...."
21. **Subject/Verb Agreement:** hedges that separate
22. **Plural of Nouns:** Russells
23. **Verb Tense:** that was
24. **Capitalization (First Word of Direct Quotation):** "They....
25. **Comma Usage (Introductory Adverb Clause):** waiting,

How to Use the Library Book/Independent Reading Literature/Reading Skills Project

1. This assignment is particularly useful as a **review** before **state-mandated reading/literature tests** and can be done using an in-class novel or an individual **library book**. Or...

2. Use the assignment simply as a review of reading/literature terms at the end of a **unit.**

3. One **advantage** to the assignment is that students can play **"Musical Chairs"** with their final projects. Ask students to leave their completed projects at their desks. All students will take paper and pen/pencil with them as they travel to various desks in the room, answering the questions from the student's project on the desk where they have moved. Answers can be checked using the author's answer sheet. **Problem questions** can be discussed as a class.

4. Students may be **assigned skills** or use problem-area skills from their individual **tally list.**

5. **Student excerpts** follow that can be given to students as practice with various skills and as samples of the assignment.

Name:____________________ **Class:**__________ **Date:**__________

Library Book/Independent Reading Literature/Reading Skills Project

Bibliographic Entry:____

____

____

Due Date of Project:______________________________________

Objectives: individualized **review of literature/reading skills** & class review of skills.

Assignment:

1. Using your **library book** and your **tally** of your individual literature/reading **problem areas**, choose **two skills** to review (**e.g.,** cause/effect, fact/non-fact, sequencing, main idea, summary, predicting outcomes/drawing logical conclusions, making generalizations, evaluating/making judgments, author's point of view, context clues, persuasive devices, specialized technical terms).

2. Compose a sample **multiple-choice question** for each skill, providing **four possible answers**.

3. In order to do this, you will need to provide a **sample passage** that gives the necessary information for your classmates to answer your questions.

   A. You may **quote passages** from the book, giving **attribution** through an internal footnote, which is the author's last name and page number, or...

   B. you may **summarize sections** in your own words.

   FOR INSTANCE, YOU MIGHT WANT TO QUOTE EXAMPLES OF FACT/NON-FACT, BUT YOU WOULD WANT TO SUMMARIZE EVENTS IN ORDER FOR YOUR CLASSMATES TO ANSWER A SEQUENTIAL-ORDER QUESTION.

4. You will need to include a **separate answer sheet** that explains the **reasoning behind each answer**--incorrect as well as correct answers.

5. You may do an extra skill and question for **extra credit.**

Name:______________________________ **Class:**_______________ **Date:**____________

Literature/Reading Skills Project Student Samples

The following are student samples of individual literature/reading skills problems. Circle the best answer.

1. "Robin sat down and began drawing with her blue pen. She added a few drops of water at the bottom so no one would think the ice cube was just a square. Then, in her best calligraphy, she wrote AKG in the center. Tentatively, she held it up for Veronica to see" **(Queen of the Sixth Grade, Cooper 10).**

Sequence--What does Robin do after she wrote AKG?

A. She held it up.
B. She sat down.
C. She added a few drops of water.
D. She looked at it.

2. "The bear had been Dawn's first teddy when she was a baby. One glass eye was missing and his fuzz had been ripped off in several places" **(I Want To Live 8).**

Summary--What is the best summary of this passage?

A. Dawn remembers the appearance of her first teddy bear.
B. Dawn tells why she wants to throw away her bear.
C. The bear has a furry tummy.
D. Dawn likes her bear.

3. "The milkweed seed twirled...down the stairs....I can do that too. Georgie put the milkweed pod back in the pocket of her red overalls. Two big jumps. Just floating...Georgie lay in a heap at the bottom of the stairs...."**(The Fledgling, Langton 5).**

Inference--From this paragraph you can infer that Georgie

A. Likes milkweed pods.
B. Wants to fly.
C. Wants to kill herself.
D. Likes stairs.

4. "They had almost reached the top of Ogden Butte when they had spotted a cougar....Both Jay and his father had jumped out of the jeep and started up the rocky mountain face. Dad was about twenty feet ahead of Jay, snapping pictures like crazy, when his feet shot out from under him....Jay had watched helpless as his father had plunged past him down the mountainside" **(Shadow of the Shaman, St. George 12).**

Sequence--According to the passage, what happened right after Jay and his father got out of the jeep and went up the mountainside?

A. Jay watched his father roll down the mountain.
B. They spotted a cougar.
C. The father died.
D. The father was taking pictures and his feet came out from underneath him.

5. "He had been enchanted with the hour, and the town, and he had felt very powerful, like the magic man with the marionettes who strung destinies across a stage on spider threads" **("At Midnight in the Month of June," Bradbury 73).**

Context Clue--In this paragraph the <u>marionettes</u> means

A. A pizza
B. A fly
C. A small jointed figure manipulated by strings, wires, or rods
D. A magic act performed all the time

6. "Yellow lace curtains hung in the windows, and red geraniums bloomed in the wooden flower box, faded and covered with a layer of rich green moss. Everything bore signs of a tranquil passage (through) time.... I took a deep breath and realized how grateful I should be to walk without a fear on such a peaceful old street" **(Echoes of the White Giraffe, Choi 5).**

Opinion--Which of the following is an opinion?

A. "Yellow lace curtains hung in the windows."
B. Red geraniums were growing in the flower boxes.
C. The street was peaceful.
D. The window boxes were covered with moss.

Fact--Which of the following is a fact in this passage?

A. "Everything bore signs of a tranquil passage through time."
B. "Yellowed lace curtains hung in the windows."
C. Pusan, Korea, is a tranquil place.
D. Red geraniums bloomed in gardens.

7. " 'For a while she did very well,' he went on. 'But later, she had to sell the cattle and the horses. She had only one old horse and some chickens now. She must be very poor, but she will not take any money from me.'" **(Mystery Ranch, Warner 13).**

Main Idea--What is the main idea of the paragraph above?

A. She has some chickens now.
B. She won't take money from her grandfather.
C. She has one old horse.
D. She's very poor.

8. "...those footprints were now as alien to him as something from a prehistoric age. They had ben made a million years ago by some other man on some other business; they were not part of him at all" **("At Midnight in the Month of June," Bradbury 181).**

Context Clue--**What does <u>prehistoric</u> mean in this passage?**

A. Something from long, long ago, as in millions of years ago.
B. Something different.
C. Something that belongs to someone else.
D. Muddy footprints.

9. "...and nailed me square in my right eye" **(Heart of a Champion, Deuker, 17).**

Drawing Conclusions--**After reading this quote, you can conclude that**

A. He probably got a black eye.
B. He could see better after the hit.
C. He was proud of himself.
D. He went to the hospital.

10. "She stood against the door. If moonlight could have struck in upon her, she would have shimmered like a small pool of water...." **("At Midnight in the Month of June,"Bradbury 174).**

Inference--**From this passage you can infer that**

A. She was drinking a Coke.
B. She had been crying.
C. She was cooking.
D. She was going to sleep.

Answers to:

Literature/Reading Skills Student Samples

1. A
2. A
3. B
4. D
5. C
6. C (opinion); B (fact)
7. D
8. A
9. A
10. B

How to Use the Book Review

1. **Bring to class** (or assign students to clip as homework) **several reviews of current books for the class to study. Ask small groups to assess the components of each review and to evaluate what made the review interesting and what kinds of facts about the books were revealed.**

2. **Use the Sample Book Reviews for models of types of** introductions, characterizations, themes, and conclusions.

3. **Assign students to do a review of their latest library book or an in-class reading.**

4. **Students enjoy writing a letter to the author as a variation of the book review. The assignment could require** quotations from the text **used as support,** blending of quotations **with the student's own words, and the usage of** internal footnotes. **With the added requirements the activity becomes a good review of or introduction to literary analysis.**

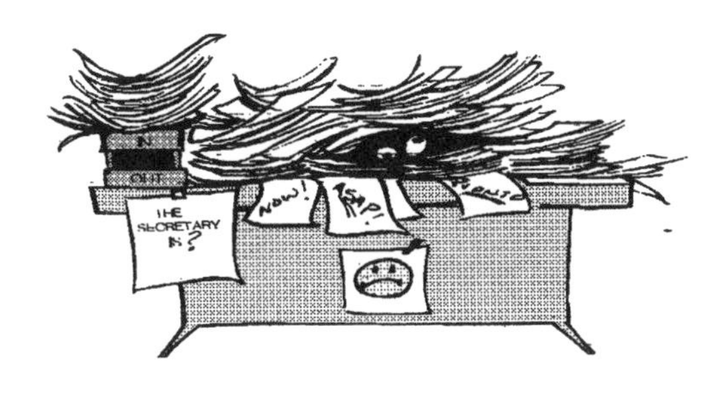

NAME________________________ CLASS______________________ DATE__________________

Sample Book Reviews

Study the sample parts of several book reviews to serve as models for your own.

Introductions:

Book Review #1: **"I can't imagine a more winning or perceptive guide to the delights, perils, cruelties, injustices, and muddles of motherhood than Mary Kay Blakely" (American Mom, reviewed by Celia Morris).**

Teacher Analysis: Appeals to mothers in a humorous, yet realistic manner, as all mothers know the "delights," but this book promises "perils, cruelties, injustices, and muddles"--in other words, what mothers usually have to wait to discuss over coffee with their best friends.

Book Review #2: **"Four years ago, when I reviewed If I Ever Return, Pretty Peggy-O, the first in Sharyn McCrumb's Ballad Series about Hamelin, a small town in the Tennessee Appalachians, I warned readers that they should read for atmosphere and character rather than `mystery.'**

"Two years ago, when I reviewed The Hangman's Beautiful Daughter, the second in the series, I was too caught up in the novel to warn readers about anything other than not to miss an accomplished writer.

"Now I have the pleasure of saying that McCrumb's world of mists, myths and murders is again waiting for you. This is a terrifically engaging book. (She

<u>Walks These Hills</u>, reviewed by Kathye Self Bergin)

Teacher Analysis: An unusual introduction in that it uses the repetition for effect regarding "warning the reader," which is in itself an attention-getter. Most readers will be drawn to instead of repelled by something with a "warning."

Book Review #3: "Fran Lebowitz escapes her tomes for adults with <u>Mr. Chas and Lisa Sue Meet the Pandas</u>, her first children's book. It is, in a word, wonderful." (reviewed by Jane P. Marshall)

Teacher Analysis: Implies that this book is an "escape" from everything that is adult and is a departure from the "scholarly" and an entry into the whimsy of childhood.

Characterization:

Book Review #1: **"Because the real life of mothers bears little resemblance to the one in most books and articles, Blakely came to depend on the coffee klatch for help from canny, sometimes nutty women who confessed their own frailties: One had gone off and left her children at the store; another had fed her baby calamine lotion instead of Pepto-Bismol; yet another woke at night to find her child strapped into the high chair where she'd abandoned her."**

Teacher Analysis: *Notice the specific details to which mothers could relate (e.g., women who actually confess that they are not "Supermom" and calamine lotion and Pepto-Bismol and being so tired babies can actually be forgotten at times) and the stylistic device of magic 3 (e.g,. One...another...yet another).*

Book Review #2: **"Sabrina Harkryder, a mountain girl whose contemporary destiny is to re-enact Katie Wyler's tragedy (things being much less changed than one might imagine), hears Katie's voice as she stumbles bravely, sometimes pathetically, toward home in the hills."**

Teacher Analysis: Readers can often relate to a character real enough to be "brave" and "pathetic" all in one day.

Book Review #3 **"Mr. Chas is a wise seven-year-old who wears glasses `because reading so many books took a lot of the juice out of my eyes and put it in my brain' and who has common sense ('It's not in the dictionary but I'm pretty sure it's doing things without mistakes caused by too much excitement').**

"He also has a best friend named Lisa. Lisa `loves plans so much that she sometimes makes them for things that don't even need them.' And she gets to boss the planning because, as she often tells Mr. Chas, she has the briefcase.

Teacher Analysis: Humor is a strong appeal, and readers can envision this "wise," glasses-wearing, book-reading child with the "juice" gone from his eyes, and his cohort Lisa sounds like Many women, the ones who not only own the "briefcases" and have the "plans" but the ones who have the gumption to make it all happen.

THEMES:

Book Review #1: **"So Blakely rejects the `national game of Let's Pretend' that perfect mothers live in perfect families, as well as the guilt-ridden notion that mothers are primarily responsible for what their children become. `More than any other part of my life,' she sees with breathtaking clarity, `being a mother taught me what it means to be human.'"**

Teacher Analysis: Readers like themes about being "human," not the "perfect" this or the perfect that to which no one can live up to anyway. Coupled with that theme is the relief that children are their own people who build their own lives and are not successes or failures "primarily" because of the Mother Factor.

Book Review #3: **"Lebowitz captures an essence of childhood, the spirit too often unappreciated and unnurtured. Her children have, as children do, escaped into a place they have made themselves, a place away from horror and stress, a place away from TV and nagging parents. A place where finding a stash of candy in the pantry is the most important thing, which, at times, it is."**

Teacher analysis: What a great theme--the pursuit and capture of the elusive nature of childhood. Grown-ups want to relieve it; children want simply to revel in it.

Conclusions:

Book Review #1: **"Uneasily proud that despite a gutsy and unconventional life she's never been arrested, Blakely is nonetheless haunted by the notion that perhaps she should have been. But motherhood, blessedly, has left her prematurely wise while cultivating a lively sense of humor and inspiring a fine and important book."**

Teacher Analysis: Again, an appeal to mothers--or readers in general--who admire "a gutsy and unconventional life," one with a dose of "lively...humor."

Book Review #2: **"She Walks These Hills, like McCrumb's two earlier Ballad novels, combines suspense--a manhunt, a vicious murder, a missing infant...--with meditations on history and memory's fracturing effect on the present. (Possibly part of the theme)**

"As with her earlier books, McCrumb juggles multiple plots with skill and grace, always reminding us that the core of her novels has to do with those whose primary identity is as an isolate from society.

She's very good. And so is this novel."

Teacher Analysis: This appeal is in its summation of the action--stated in a magic 3. Readers who like "multiple plots" and the suspense often associated with those "isolate(d) from society" will read this conclusion, remember its effectiveness, and run to the nearest bookstore.

Book Review #3: **"As Mr. Chas might say, it is definitely true that having more Mr. Chas and Lisa Sue adventures is a happy thought instead of a sad one."**

Teacher Analysis: Using a character from the novel to speak to readers about his "happy adventures" is a "novel" testimony, one that no doubt will attract attention and develop a whole new audience waiting for more.

Brooke Baker
Book Review
Letter to the Author

Dear Mr. Cadnum,

Your novel, Taking It, was absolutely wonderful! My personal favorite parts were so great that I just had to tell someone, so I called my mom. This is how the conversation went:

"You won't believe what's happening in the story I'm reading!"

"What?"

"Well, first Anna, Maureen's best friend, plays mind games with the manager of the corner store and the police! Then, she gets caught. The store manager decides that she believes Anna stole something so she calls her into her office."

"Was she scared?"

"Let me finish, Mom! Anna goes in and finds out that she has been accused of shoplifting. Sure, Anna had had a problem three years ago when she went on a stealing spree and couldn't stop taking things. She isn't stealing this time; she's teasing. The red and bluish-green scarf she's tormenting the police with is placed back on the shelf where it came from. But, the police find a green, yellow, and white painted scarf in her purse."

"Do you mean she doesn't even know she's stealing?"

"Exactly! She'd done it so many times that she has no clue she's even doing it. The police let her go because the manager and Anna's father are close friends."

"Poor Anna! Does her father get her help?"

"He tries, but it doesn't work. They join a class, but it's useless. They do it again as a father/daughter thing. When the therapy doesn't work, she's forced to move to her mom and stepdad's house. They're hoping that might help."

"Wow, Brooke, have you written to the author since this happened?"

"Yes, I've been waiting for him to respond. I know he has a lot of fans."

"Well, if you find out anything, call me back."

"Why, Mom, do you have something important to do?"

"Yes, I saw that book at Walden. I've got to get it!"

That was our conversation, Mr. Cadnum. My mom liked your story as much as I did. The only thing I didn't like was that you haven't made a sequel.

Your pleased reader,

Brooke Baker

Brooke Baker

Nikki Carroll
Book Review
Letter to the Author

Thank You

Dear Ms. Hesse:

April 2, Library Day. While listening to our librarian in the background, I walked over and pulled Karen Hesse's *Letters from Rifka* off the shelf. Then I didn't know what I was getting myself into, but now I know that this is not just a plain library book for me to check out and hide behind in class while talking to my neighbor, but instead a book that deep down has a meaning to all people, even those who don't have blonde hair or don't practice the Jewish religion or aren't named "Rifka."

This book has caught me by the collar and held me down to read it, though I must admit I haven't tried to fight it off, for I have wanted to stay and see what it is all about. And one of the best things that your book contains is a book inside a book, the Pushkin inside the letters or should I say the letters inside the Pushkin.

When Rifka, a twelve-year-old Jew, says she is American-bound, she means it no matter what obstacles she has to overcome. Rifka suffers all kinds of hardships, but in the end gets to where she wants to be. Rifka is a brave girl, who is apparently not scared of anything, but on the inside she is small girl with fears of her life in the present and her life in the future. Rifka wouldn't be classified as immature or indifferent or insensitive, but independent, a trait to which many of us should aspire.

Now as I finish up on page 148, I understand what you have kept trying to tell me. Never will I look at the world with the same hate-filled eyes, as now I have a new perspective, a new outlook, a new viewpoint. Rifka makes me realize that my life would be a dream world for her and probably many others like her. It is encouraging to see that someone could endure so much pain and suffering.

I thank you for the book you have written, I thank Aunt Lucy for the story she has told, and I thank God for the ability He has given you to write with such grace and reality. Though I am not Tovah, I have enjoyed the letters written from Rifka.

Sincerely,

Nikki Carroll

Nikki Carroll

Marcus McDaniel
Book Review
Letter to the Author

Dear Mr. Herring:

Today, as I pulled the book The Leaving Summer off the shelf, I saw myself on the cover looking into the face of the escaped convict on Yankee Hill two summers ago. I remember it, plain as day, when Daddy brought home the convicts to help in the tomato patch. I remember the "one blond man tumbling from the front seat of the pickup (and) a second, older-looking one jumping from the flat bed" (2). I remember Mrs. Dixie saying "'Men with tattoos are dangerous'" (3) and being scared half to death of them. I remember when the convict waited hot and sweaty for some water "with one tattered boot inside the door, waiting in that position...while I drew the water" (8-9).

It was Aunt Ada and I who "fought our way up the familiar hill, which had turned foreign in the night rain," (66) while trying to get to the wounded convict and bring him home. I remember when "we bent down on either side of the man, and at Aunt Ada's instruction I lifted his arm around my neck," (68) the man soaked with water and covered with leaves, dirt, and scratches. I was there when Aunt Ada told me "'to hold the skin together while she stitched it'" (72).

I remember the day "Aunt Ada sat on the porch wearing the kimono she'd bought in Tokyo," (134) waiting on Bass to go to the dance on Friday. When Friday came, Bass ran from the basement into the back seat and "struggled onto the floor between the front and back seat," (140) so as not to be seen by anyone who would recognize him. I can remember the "hands (that) clapped down hard on my shoulders," (144) just as I started to get up to go to the cake walk with a girl.

Thank you, Mr. Herring, for helping me remember Aunt Ada, Miss Dixie, Daddy, Mama, and Bass after two years of being stowed away in the back of my mind. After reading your book The Leaving Summer, I remembered. I remembered it all.

Your reader,

Marcus McDaniel

Marcus McDaniel

How to Use Library Tests

1. The **Research Quiz** is a generic quiz over such **research concepts** as outlining, footnoting, blending quotes, bibliographic information, and actual topical researched facts learned.

   ✏It can be given **after the final draft** of the research paper has been completed as a **cumulative test** or **before the draft is competed as a reminder** to students of correct research procedures.

2. The **Research Test** is a 50-question, true/false scantron test covering writing note cards, outlining/webbing, writing rough and final drafts, proofreading/revising, and using bibliographic information correctly.

   ✏This test could be given **before or after the final research draft is completed.**

3. The **Library Book Literary Terms Application Test** is included as one method of testing students over their **individual library books**. The test is designed to complement class study of literary terms and to provide students with the opportunity to practice using quoted material from the text (complete with internal footnotes) as support.

   ✏Students could be given **two weeks to read their books** outside of class and then a **day for testing.**

Name:______________________ Class:______________ Date:__________

Research Quiz

Answer the following questions in complete sentences.

1. **A.** Explain what it means to use **parallel structure** in an outline.

____

____

____

B. Give an example of an outline that is in parallel structure with **two Roman numerals** and **two subcategories** for each Roman numeral.

____

____

____

2. Give an example of an **internal footnote.** To do this, make up some information that could have been taken from research and then create a footnote that gives attribution for this information.

____

____

____

3. **A.** Explain what you have learned about **blending quoted material** from a text.

____

____

____

B. Give an example of a blended quote.

4. A. Explain when you would use a **quote within a quote**.

B. Give an example of a quote within a quote that could appear in a research paper.

5. Explain what a **bibliography** or a **Works Cited** is.

6. Put the following information into a **bibliographic format:**

Title of book: Dandelion Wine
Author: Ray Bradbury
Publishing Company: Bantam
Places of Publication: New York/Toronto/London/Sydney
Copyright Dates: 1946, 1947, 1952

✔Remember what you have learned regarding multiple places of publication and copyright dates.

---

7. Write a **paragraph** explaining what you have learned while doing your research paper. Be sure to **include three things learned.** Follow the following format:

1st sentence: topic sentence
2nd sentence: 1st thing learned
3rd sentence: support
4th sentence: 2nd thing learned
5th sentence: support
6th sentence: 3rd thing learned
7th sentence: support
8th sentence: conclusion

✔You will be graded on **being specific, following the formula, and proofreading.**

✔When you are finished, put **brackets** around your topic and concluding sentences, **circle** your transition words, and **box in** your main ideas.

Sample answers to:

Research Quiz

1.

A. **All equal parts of the outline** (i.e., Roman numerals) **must be stated using the same parts of speech** (e.g., nouns).

B. I. **Dogs as guardians** (noun)
- A. **With children** (prepositional phrase)
- B. **With the epileptic** (prepositional phrase)

II. **Dogs as lifesavers** (noun)
- A. **With rescue teams** (prepositional phrase)
- B. **With law enforcement** (prepositional phrase)

2. **For people in nursing homes, the dogs are a source of therapy and comfort** (Lagoni 347).

3.

A. **Material quoted from a text cannot stand alone; it must be blended with the student author's own words.**

B. **Physical punishment of a child causes the adult to "create within that child a mistrust" in others** (Barbour 68).

4.

A. **A quotation within a quotation is used to quote a phrase that is already in quotation marks** (e.g., dialogue, titles that use quotation marks, etc.).

B. **I thought,** "WHAT KIND OF PLACE IS THIS TO FIGURE HIGH-SPEED MATH? 'IF A BUSHEL OF WHEAT MAKES 315 LOAVES OF BREAD EACH WEIGHING ONE POUND TWO OUNCES, HOW MANY LOAVES OF THIS WEIGHT CAN BE MADE WITH 473 BUSHELS OF WHEAT?'" (Example from a narrative research paper)

5. **A Bibliography or Works Cited is a list of sources used in a research paper.**

6. **Bradbury, Ray. Dandelion Wine. New York: Bantam, 1952.**

7. **Answers will vary.**

Research Test

Do not write on the test. Answer on scantron:
A=True; B=False.

Note Cards

1. When taking all note cards, you should quote all information exactly from your source so that you can put it in your own words later in the paper.

2. "Slugs" are the author's name put on the back of the note cards for easy reference.

3. A source card for a magazine would include the title of the article, the month and year the magazine was published, and the page number(s) on which the article appears.

4. A source card for an encyclopedia includes the volume number but not the title of the article.

5. For a source card with more than two authors, the rule is the same as for one author: last name, first name.

6. Letters of the alphabet can be used in succession on source cards and corresponding note cards so that all the source card information will not have to be put on each note card.

7. Each note card should include a page number.

Outline/Web

8. If you wanted to make a web of your topic listing three main aspects or ideas you wanted to cover in your paper, you would put your topic in a central circle and draw three circles coming off the central circle, like spokes.

9. If you made an outline of your topic and had a Roman numeral one (I), then you must have a Roman numeral two (II).

10. To indicate subdivisions of Roman numerals in an outline (in other words, information you would include in that area), you would use Arabic numbers so that your outline would look like the following:

I.
  1.
  2.

Rough Draft

11. For the beginning stages of a rough draft, you need to get your ideas down on paper even if your spelling, sentence structure, punctuation, etc. are not correct yet.

12. When you summarize in your own words ideas or information from a source, you should document that source either in the summary itself or in a footnote.

13. A footnote includes the author's last name, first name, name of source, and page number.

14. A footnote that comes at the end of a sentence is put in parentheses with a period after the parentheses.

Revising/Proofreading

15. After you have written your rough draft, you need to reread it to see if there are any major revisions that need to be done before you actually proofread for technical errors such as spelling, etc.

16. The rule for paragraphing dialogue is to start a new paragraph for each new speaker.

17. The following dialogue is correctly punctuated:

"She said, They won't reject the plan."

18. This dialogue is correctly punctuated:

"You know what you meant to say," the instructor remarked "but the reader doesn't".

19. This dialogue is correct:

Rice is the major food of all Asian people, "Mary said."

20. The four ways to correct a run-on sentence are a period, comma , semicolon, and clause signal (i.e. since, because, etc.).

21. The following sentence is correctly punctuated:

My grades are good, my social life isn't.

22. The following sentence is correctly punctuated:

I like people, and they like me.

23. One possible way to correct the following sentence is to add the word when.

I don't do my work I am punished by my parents.

24. A fragment is always a short sentence.

25. The following is not a fragment:

Walking down the street in my new leather boots and my "who-cares" attitude, whistling away, checking out who is there to be seen.

26. The following is a fragment:

My father, my idol, the first man to give me flowers, the first man to care.

27. One of the following sentences is a fragment:

I was afraid of my basketball coach. A stern and sarcastic man. He was never satisfied with my ability.

28. One way to correct a fragment is to attach it to the preceding or the following sentence.

29. Both of the following are sentences:

I thought my friend and I would be killed. When the motorcycle hit us from behind.

30. The following is not a fragment:

As a child, I went to the beach with the people who lived next door.

31. The following sentence has no error in verb tense:

The kid parked his bicycle in the driveway, so his dad runs over it and becomes furious as a result.

32. There is no error in verb tense:

We had already ordered the materials when we decided not to build a gazebo after all.

33. There is an error in verb tense:

How ironic that a Houston doctor wrote books on being healthy. Then, she dies of lung cancer due to years of smoking.

34. There is no error in verb tense:

Last year Mama went to work, Daddy goes on a diet, and I am going crazy.

35. If your narrative starts in past tense, it should stay in past tense unless there is a reason for the verb tense to shift.

36. One way to tell if sentences need to be combined is the unnecessary repetition of words (words that are repeated **not** for effect).

37. The following sentences need to be combined:

The trees were covered in ice. The trees seemed to glow in the sunlight.

38. These sentences need to be combined:

The boys stole money from the office. They were expelled from school.

39. One way to combine sentences is to use an appositive such as the following sentence:

Ethel, my best friend, is working on her research paper.

40. Spelling of homophones (words that sound the same but have different spellings) should be checked just as thoroughly as the spelling of more "complicated" words.

41. Their means they are.

42. Its shows possession.

43. To means very or also.

Final Copy

44. The order of the final copy of a research paper is as follows: cover sheet, bibliography, outline, scratch copy, and final copy.

45. When typed, a final copy is always double-spaced.

Bibliography/Works Cited

46. Bibliographies should be alphabetized by the last name of the author or, if there is no author given, by the first thing to appear on the entry itself, such as the article title.

47. Bibliographic entries should be numbered.

48. Periods are used at the end of each bibliographic entry.

49. The first line of each bibliographic entry is indented three spaces

50. A bibliography lists all sources whether they appear as documentation in the paper or not.

Answers to:

Research Test

1.	B	21.	B	41.	B
2.	B	22.	A	42.	A
3.	A	23.	A	43.	B
4.	B	24.	B	44.	B
5.	B	25.	B	45.	A
6.	A	26.	A	46.	A
7.	A	27.	A	47.	B
8.	A	28.	A	48.	A
9.	A	29.	B	49.	B
10.	B	30.	A	50.	B
11.	A	31.	B		
12.	A	32.	A		
13.	B	33.	A		
14.	A	34.	B		
15.	A	35.	A		
16.	A	36.	A		
17.	B	37.	A		
18.	B	38.	A		
19.	B	39.	A		
20.	B	40.	A		

NAME:____ CLASS_______________________ DATE_______________

Library Book
Literary Terms Application Test

Assignment:

a. All answers must be in complete sentences, or points will be deducted.

B. For answers that require quotes from the text, quotation marks and page numbers must be used, or points will be deducted.

C. Answer the following questions about your library book. You may use no notes, but you may refer to the text itself.

1. **SETTING :** Quote the setting of the story. Remember that setting contains two elements.

____

____

____

2. PLOT: **Draw a** plot graph **below. Graph the action of the story by listing at least** five rising actions, one climax, **and** one falling action. **Remember to list events of importance and to list them** sequentially.

3. CONFLICT :

a. Quote **an example of** primary conflict **in the story.**

____

____

____

b. Explain **whether the example quoted is** internal **or** external.

____

____

____

4. COMPARISON/CONTRAST:

a. Quote **an example of the most important** comparison or contrast **in the story.**

b. Explain the comparison or contrast.

5. **THEME:** If the theme is stated in the story, quote it. If not, explain it in your own words.

6. **DESCRIPTION:**

a. Quote an effective descriptive passage.

b. Explain why this is an effective description.

C. Quote a figurative language device **and** identify its type.

1. Quote: ______________________________

____

____

2. Type: ______________________________

7. Rating: Rate this book on a scale of 1 (low) -10 (high) **and explain your rating** using three specific examples from the book.

A. Rating: __________

B. Explanation:

1. ______________________________

____

____

2. ______________________________

____

____

3. ______________________________

How to Combine Vocabulary Usage, Research, and Letter /Post Card Writing

1. Using the class's current **vocabulary words**, assign a certain number to be used in writing a **post card** to parents, a friend, family member, etc.

2. Ask students to include **two** (or any designated number) **researched facts** in their writing.

3. You may also assign a certain number of **"smiley-face tricks"** (see "Smiley-Face Tricks") **to be included** (e.g., specific details for effect, similes, metaphors, repetition for effect, etc.).

4. Assign **internal footnotes** and **bibliographic entries** as a review.

TEACHER MODEL
LETTER INCLUDING VOCABULARY WORDS

DEAR DAD,

Just a note from your I-wish-I-didn't-have-to-go-to-Colorado daughter. Wasn't there some ancient TV program from your day and age with some completely **erroneous** and sexist title like "Father Knows Best"? Well, I never watched it and didn't like the obvious premise, especially since at our house it's some unspoken law anyway, as we all know--your knowing best, that is. I can just hear you now. You'd say "the truth hurts," and I'd say something "**Socrates**esque" like "what is truth" and stare **existentially** out some hopefully handy window. Anyway thought you'd like to know that at least in this case you've been **vindicated.** I'm only going to say this once so don't get used to it, but--okay--you were right. It pains me to write the words, but we're finally here in Colorado, and I already love it!

When I looked up from my reading of <u>The Inferno</u>, which I had chosen especially for this trip, suddenly to my right there were the most awesome mountains and guys climbing those mountains and to my left more mountains and more guys and, oh yeah, some **serpentine** rivers or streams or whatever and, oh yeah, some cute guys fly-fishing. Glad I decided to make the trip after all, what with all those mountains and rivers. I can already see what an **edifying** experience it will be.

I will tell you, though, that Allison almost drove us all nuts with her constant **litany** of questions: "Why couldn't I bring a friend?" and " How many more miles to the next (fill in the blank) bathroom? motel with a pool? hotel with Leonardo DiCapprio?" and "Do you like my nails Brandy Wine or Tequila Sunrise?" No one cared about color--we were only praying we'd stay alive to see her final choice since she almost asphyxiated us removing nail and toenail polish on the hour for at least eight hours. Do you realize that's 160 **phalanges**--Claudia and I figured it out--and you wonder how bored we were. Anyway, Mother and Aunt Maxine said they liked the wine and tequila parts but told her to get a grip, which she promptly did on Claudia's and my necks. Something about her own version of the Heimlich maneuver and Walker, Texas Ranger's most successful move. When Claudia's windpipe eventually resumed its natural shape, she wheezed something to the effect that Allison should be strapped to the top of the car like Chevy Chase's dead mother-in-law or great-aunt or whatever she was in whatever movie that was. As for me, I kept wondering--as much as one is able to **posit** any theory with a massive migraine due to whiplash--what possessed you and Mom to provide me with a sibling. You know what a **recluse** I am. And truly, Dad, one isn't such a lonely number after all, but I guess it's too late for that. More tomorrow...

* * *

Second day here and you're my idol! Mom said Claudia and I could escape Allison-induced **purgatory** and set off an excursion of our own. It was like we were two women warriors in search of the Holy Grail or Sasquatch or at the very least a yummy mocha cappuccino. And guess what? The Grail and Sasquatch will have to wait, but we did sip the best mocha this side of the Rockies with Alsace, a gorgeous grad student from Kent, England. I knew this trip would do me a world of good. More later....

Your lovin'-every-minute-of-this-trip daughter,

Ellen

Letter
Including Sample Researched Information

Research and Letter Writing

We're finally here in Colorado--yeah--the home of pygmy forests, semi-arid deserts, and elevations varying from 3,387 feet to 14,433 feet **(18-19).** At least that's the stuff Mom kept announcing as she'd turn another page in her travel book. While she droned on about pinion juniper woodlands--whatever they are--I was wondering about what Colorado had in the way of guys. Talk about generation gap! Anyway, after two more chapters of trees and sand, I somehow warmed to the idea ....

Bibliographic Entry:

Litvak. Colorado Travel Smart Trip Planner. Santa Fe: John Muir, 1996.

...we did sip the best mocha this side of the Rockies with Alsace, a gorgeous grad student from Kent, England. Now this guy's a fellow after my own heart. We talked food--Did I know that Thackhery's House Restaurant was where William Makepeace Thackery wrote Turnbridge Toys **(295)**? Fascinating! And shopping--I simply must visit the Pantiles, a colonnaded walkway of some sort just filled with shops **(294)**! Wonder how much of an advance I could get on my allowance? And then there's sightseeing--not all those boring trees, but the "loveliest castle in the world," Leeds Castle, also known as a "literary salon" during the early 1600's **(287).** Jordan says if I visit him we could go on an excursion? Wow! Sure beats the mall. Guess what, when I was talking to him....

Bibliographic Entry:

Porter, Darwin and Danforth Prince. Frommer's '98 England. New York: Macmillan, 1998.

Note and Bibliographic Cards on Kent, England, and Colorado

Note Card #1--Kent, England

Leeds Castle	287
"literary salon" -- 1st half of 17th cent.	

Note Card #2--Kent, England

	287
Leeds Castle --Ben Jonson inspired to write one of his best poems	

Note Card #3--Kent, England

	292
Leeds Castle	
"loveliest castle in the world"	

Note Card #4--Kent, England

294

Pantiles, colonnaded walkway for shoppers, tea drinkers, and diners

Note Card #5--Kent, England

295

Thackery's House Restaurant--once inhabited by William Makepeace Thackery--wrote Turnbridge Toys here

Bibliographic Card--Kent, England

Porter, Darwin and Danforth Prince. Frommer's '98 England. New York: Macmillan, 1998.

Note Card #1--Colorado

18
Colorado--semi-arid desert found at elevations of

Note Card #2--Colorado

18
Pinion-juniper woodlands--pygmy forests--trees are stunted

Note Card #3--Colorado

19
Colorado--lowest level= 3,387 feet hightest=14,433 feet

NOTE AND BIBLIOGRAPHIC CARDS

Bibliographic Card--Colorado

Litvak, Dianna. Colorado Travel Smart Trip Planner. Santa Fe: John Muir, 1996.

How to Use the Survival Dictionary

1. The purpose of the **Survival Dictionary** is not only to encourage students to look at words differently, to add their own "slants" to words--thus providing opportunities to practice writing for a specified audience (e.g., their peers)--but also to give students more practice with using the dictionary as a **"research" tool.**

2. The **Survival Dictionary** can be made more complex if students are asked to research and include in their "definitions" such information as etymologies, syllabication, pronunciations, plural forms of nouns, principal parts of verbs, comparisons of adjectives and adverbs, cross-references, synonyms, etc.

3. Students can identify their **five or ten best entries** to be read aloud to the class. The best five dictionaries could receive extra credit or win class prizes.

Excerpts from Jerad Norris:

Deranged--(adj.) As in the principal that evilly snickers as he throws out detentions, and the teachers that violently slam wooden yardsticks onto cringing desks.

Edible--(adj.) As not in the pink-and-white mush handed to you by a mysterious yellow-gloved hand on a black-and-white speckled tray on Mystery Monday in the lunch room.

King--(noun) As in the 200-pound, gorilla-like, hair-covered football lineman headed straight for you, his mouth growling and slobbering.

Marshall--(noun) As in the cop that enjoys roaming the halls--searching, tracing, scanning for an unexpecting kid achieving something mischievous.

Oral--(adj.) As in the ten-billion-point, don't-do-it-and-fail-forever oral report that the language arts teacher assigns at least once every six weeks.

Utopia--(noun) As in the perfect school with no homework, no teachers, and no principals. A place where you can roam the halls and go to the bathroom every five minutes.

Excerpts from Amber Thomas, Liesel Smith, Warren Andrade:

Different-- (adj.) The girl in the back row of your English class, wearing the neon-green, fuzzy ball earrings, with her hair in perfect pigtails, and a polka-dot shirt, pink-and-yellow striped shorts, and orange socks.

Nickname--(noun) A term such as "speed bumps" shouted out in front of everyone, including the finest boy in school, by the donkey-faced, no-brained goofball that sits behind you in history.

Teenager--(noun) A stubborn, spoiled, hard-headed kid who won't lose an argument, who won't take "no" as an answer, and who thinks brand-new clothes should magically appear on his/her body.

Yitterlatterly--(adv.) How you walk when you feel that today you look good, you are the cream of the crop, the best pick of the bunch, there's no more sour juice in your lemon. How you swish and sway when you look fabulous, `a la Cindy Crawford.

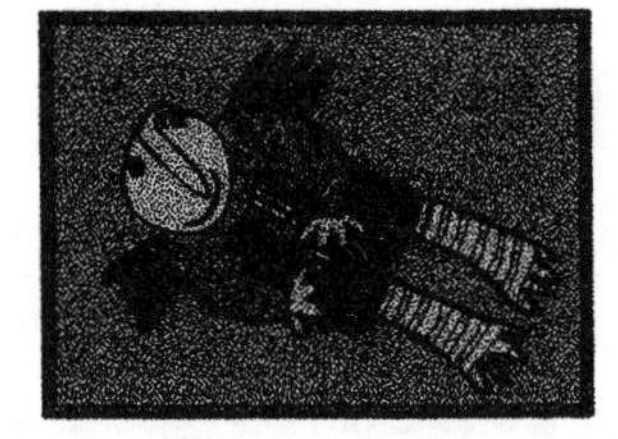

Excerpts from Nikki Carroll:

Abnormal--(adj.) What you are when you come back to school with the clothes that were popular last year because you were out of the loop a whole two-and-a-half months, and now everybody is looking at you like you're an alien.

Grades--(noun) The two-to-three digit numbers that are received from teachers as gifts for Distinguished Honor Roll students and as bombs ready to explode and blow away all fun for failing kids.

Honesty--(noun) 1. When you ask if your new sky-blue cashmere sweater looks good (when you know it's too tight, too big, too something) and your best friend confirms your fears or when you ask your friend if she were talking about you to the other girls in P.E. and she was and she admits it even if she doesn't want to. 2. A trait that rarely exists in grades 6-12.

Incompetent--(adj.) A personality trait of the dumb jock sitting next to you in American history, mistaking John Adams for the first President of the United States, always asking for paper and pencil, and never being able to do his work by himself, being more interested in the ceiling tiles than the teacher.

Kool Beans--(adj./noun) Words that you say to yourself while skipping down the hall to describe how nifty it is when you ace the science test over genetics that brings your final grade to an "A +" and allows you to get Distinguished Honor Roll.

Love--(noun) Another word for hormones going a hundred miles an hour and boys drooling over girls in short skirts and girls whispering to each other about the cutest boy's new hair cut.

Nasty--(adj.) When your friend sitting next to you in lunch turns to you and says "Hey" then opens his/her mouth to show you the outcome of an already chewed-up bite of pizza.

NAME: ______________________ CLASS: ____________ DATE: ________

Bookmarks

Assignment:

1. Summarize **your book, explaining aspects from the** beginning, middle, and end**; however, do not reveal the ending for the reader. Give only enough of the conclusion to whet the reader's appetite.**

2. Illustrate **your bookmark with** scenes, characters, **etc. from your book.**

3. **The** form **your bookmark can take could be an** oversized bookmark, a series of bookmarks to depict various chapters**, etc.**

4. **Include a** bibliographic entry **for your book.**

5. **Be prepared to** present **your bookmark to the class.**

Jessica Stephens
Bookmark

The Stalker

Living near the beaches of Corpus Christi, Jennifer Lee Wilcox's best friend's so-called "mother," Stella Trax, is strangled to death in her own home. Worse than that, the police think that Bobbie, Jennifer's friend and daughter of Stella, committed the crime. Jennifer knows that Bobbie would not kill Stella, even though they did get into screaming fights sometimes.

Jennifer is determined to find the killer so her best friend will get released from jail; therefore, she sets out to find a private investigator to help her with this huge task. Lucas Maldonado, an ex-cop, agrees to help her find Stella's real murderer.

As Jennifer starts to search for clues, someone starts to stalk her. Who is stalking Jennifer? Who killed Daryll, Stella, and Margo (one of Stella's friends)**? Who will it be: Mr. Bartlee Biddle, one of the other private eyes Jennifer tried to get to help her? Or perhaps it's Daryll, one of Bobbie's stepbrothers. Or maybe Elton, her other stepbrother, is the guilty party. Read to uncover the surprise ending.**

Corpus Christi, Texas

Locations of Crime Scenes

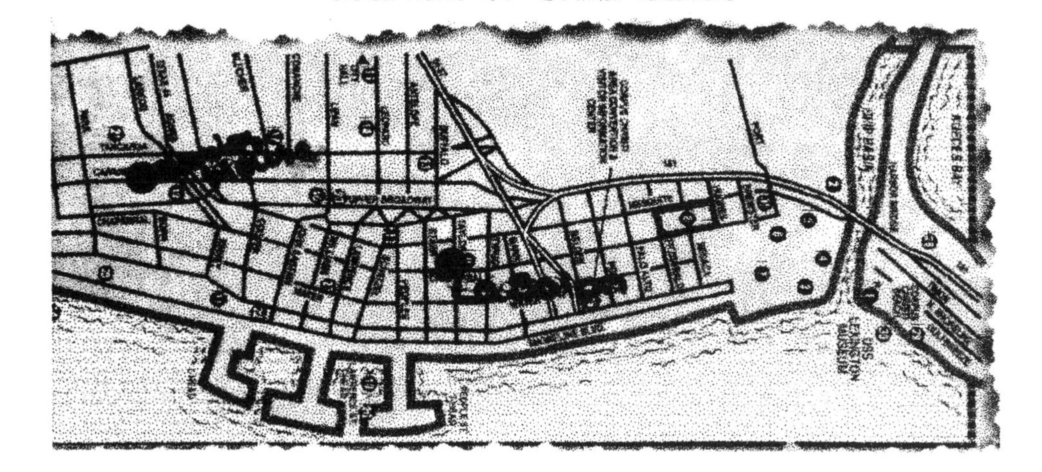

Mary Nelson
Bookmark

Ghost Horse

Callie has just moved to the Arizona desert because of her dad's transfer in job sites. After Callie has settled into her new home, she meets a girl named Amy, who has a brother that teaches horseback riding. Callie loves horses and wants to start riding right away.

One night a silver-grey horse named Star appears at Callie's window. Callie is not sure why she is the only one who can see Star and is puzzled about all the strange dreams of a boy named Michael and a horse named Star.

Callie soon figures out that one day when Michael had gone out with Star they were caught in a fire and because of Star's fear of fire she throws Michael off her back and leaves him.

Star's guilt leads Callie to a canyon to relive the tragedy. After Callie saves Michael from the burning flames, Star mysteriously disappears to live with Michael forever.

How to Use the Circle Response Sheet

1. Use the **Circle Response Sheet** as an alternative to partner or small group responses for virtually any mode of writing that is organized into aspects or points (e.g., persuasive, comparison/contrast, how-to, etc.).

2. One **advantage** is that students get practice in reading various aspects of their classmates' papers.

   A. For example, the first reader reads only the **thesis, topic sentence** for each paragraph, and the **restatement of the thesis.** The same reader on the second time around the circle reinforces his/her knowledge of these statements and topic sentences by proofreading a second author's paper.

   B. On the third time around, the reader concentrates on **introductory** and **concluding paragraphs**, thus reinforcing for the student the purpose of these parts of an essay.

   C. The next passes will include proofreading various **bodies of the essays,** providing authors with peer suggestions for revisions.

3. The teacher might find it helpful to be in the circle too, passing his/her paper around for suggestions--or using a sample paper--so that he/she can get an idea of the **progress of the class** as a whole. **Mini-lessons** on grammatical mistakes, elaboration, sentence combining, etc. can be given as needed as further **revisionary strategies** before students make their final drafts.

Name:______________________________ **Class:**______________ **Date:**____________

Circle Response Group

Assignment:

☺After students move desks into one large circle, they will pass their essays to the right. Each student will then **check for the following components** assigned to them and make any corrections on the essay itself.

☺When the teacher indicates, papers will pass again to the right until all aspects of the essay have been **proofread by several readers.**

☺This **response sheet** will be passed with the paper to which it belongs.

1. **Reader # 1 checks:**
   - A. **Thesis** (3 aspects stated in parallel terms)
   - B. **Topic sentence for each body paragraph** (transition word/phrase) + (key idea)
   - C. **Restatement of thesis** (3 aspects)

   1st reader: signature & comments:______________________________

____

____

2. **Reader #2 checks:**
Same proofreading assignment as #1

2nd reader signature & comments:______________________________

____

____

3. **Reader #3 checks:**

A. **Introductory paragraph** (Interesting beginning) + (thesis statement)

B. **Conclusion paragraph** (Interesting) + (thesis restatement)

3rd reader signature & comments:______________________________

____

____

4. **Reader #4 checks:**
Same proofreading assignment as #3

4th reader signature & comments:______________________________

____

____

5. **Reader #5 checks:**
First body

A. **Topic sentence**
B. **At least three detailed supports**

5th reader signature & comments:______________________________

____

____

CIRCLE RESPONSE GROUP 3

6. **Reader #6 checks:**
Same proofreading assignment as #5

6th reader signature & comments:____________________________________

____

____

7. **Reader #7 checks:**
Second body
- **A. Topic sentence**
- **B. At least 3 detailed supports**

7th reader signature & comments:____________________________________

____

____

8. **Reader #8 checks:**
Same proofreading assignment as #7

8th reader signature & comments:____________________________________

____

____

9. **Reader #9 checks:**
Third body
- **A. Topic sentence**
- **B. At least 3 detailed supports**

9th reader signature & comments:____________________________________

10. **Reader #10 checks:**
Same proofreading assignment as #9

10th reader signature & comments:____________________________

11. **Reader #11 checks:**
Entire essay
- **A. Grammatical errors**
- **B. Varied methods of elaboration)**

11th reader signature & comments:____________________________

12. **Reader #12 checks:**
Same assignment as #11

12 reader signature & comments:____________________________

How to Use Vocabulary Assignments

1. The "Personalized Vocabulary" assignment helps students apply vocabulary words from their novel/library book to their own lives.

   ☺ Students enjoy having a designated word count and consider it like a puzzle to be solved.

   ☺ Students also have the opportunity to practice using stylistic devices, as one "smiley-face" trick (See "Smiley-Face Tricks) must be included for each entry.

   ☺ The assignment allows students to illustrate their entries, adding another dimension to the assignment.

2. The "Personification Vocabulary Test" is a higher level application quiz asking students to make their vocabulary words "come alive."

   ☺ Since the figurative language device of personification is the focus, students must review the six methods of characterization, a reading/literature skill.

   ☺ The definitive word count is like a game for students and more "fun" than an open-ended count.

   ☺ Writing skills are integrated with vocabulary and reading skills in that students must include and identify one stylistic device and proofread for mechanical and structural errors.

3. The "Brochure Vocabulary Test" is an application/synthesis test, as it asks students to "sell" a word from their novel/library book. They must use various modes of writing--DESCRIPTION, EXPLANATION, HOW-TO, COMPARISON/CONTRAST, NARRATIVE--within their persuasive brochure.

☺ A contest can be held for the most "convincing" word or words in each class.

☺ Brochures make an interesting, informative display/bulletin board.

Name:________________ Class:____________________ Date:________________

Personalized Vocabulary

Assignment:

1. Choose five of the vocabulary words from your in-class reading and five from your library book.

2. For each vocabulary word, write 25 words (exactly 25 words) that do the following:

   a. Uses the word appropriately
   b. Spells the word correctly
   c. Explains your personal connection to the word
   d. Uses one labeled smiley-face trick

3. Five words must contain a labeled context clue

4. Each word must be illustrated (in such a way as to pictorially represent your word) by one of the following methods:

   a. Original drawing
   b. Computer graphics
   c. Magazine pictures
   d. Other--see me

5. Example: My histrionics--whether to obtain an advance on my allowance or sympathy in general--work on my father like the crocodile tears of my youth (simile).

5. The project should be put together in an **original way** using one of the following ideas:

a. Diary form
b. Pop-up book
c. Flash cards
d. Collage
e. Flip book
f. Letters/Post cards
g. Other--See me

Rubric:

1. Usage and spelling of words
2. Quality of writing/usage of labeled smiley-face trick
3. Accuracy of context clues
4. Appropriateness of pictures
5. Neatness

Due Date: ______________________________

Parent Signature: ______________________________

Bibliographic Entries on work itself!

Point Value = 300 points

Name:________________ Class:________________ Date:________________

Personification Vocabulary Test

Assignment: Using your list of vocabulary words, choose **three** to **personify.**

1. You must pretend that the word is a **person** and describe the type of person that your word would be. Remember the **six methods of characterization:** appearance, actions, speech, inner thoughts and feelings, what others say, and environment.

2. Each description must be **50 words exactly.** On your final draft, **number** above each word.

3. You must use at least **one smiley face** (that you will label) per passage.

4. Remember that the **meaning of your word must be evident** in the passage. Be sure to underline your vocabulary word.

5. You will be graded on the spelling and usage of the vocabulary word, the quality of the writing, spelling of common words, fragment- and run-on-free sentences, and your smiley faces.

Samples:

1. **Tenacity** sits at her desk, revising, proofreading, revising again. Her friends say writing is too much work, her parents say she should get out more like "normal" kids, but **Tenacity** says she's in for the long haul, and she knows she's right. Success is her goal; she'll never give up.

2. **Pathos** has been dumped again. She can't figure out what goes wrong. She has no trouble attracting guys, but as soon as she and her dates immerse themselves in a meaningful conversation, she reveals her true self--the ugly pain hidden under her beautiful mask. She smiles; they don't. *Dumped. (*Fragment for effect.)

Name:____________________ Class:____________________ Date:____________

Brochure Vocabulary Test

I. Assignment:

You are on a committee that has been asked to advertise words! You must create a brochure that appeals to the public and that sells your word. The following must be included:

A. A description of what your word looks like

B. An explanation of what your word can do

C. What three steps can be involved in your word (e.g. How to...)

D. What you can compare your word to

E. A short anecdote (story) about your word

F. Who would want to "buy" this word

II. Vocabulary Words from which to Choose:

You will choose one of the following words:

____

III. Rubric:

A. Minimum word count for entire brochure 300 words, approximately 50 words per aspect

B. Spelling and usage of your word as well as spelling in general

C. Quality of writing--at least 10 smiley-face passages for entire brochure

D. Punctuation--emphasis on comma usage

E. Picture(s) depicting your word and appropriate "decorative qualities"

F. Brochure typed and in appropriate format

IV. Extra Credit:

A. Characterization "cut-out" using one or more of your vocabulary words

B. An extra brochure using a different word

How to Use What a Character

1. **What a Character!** provides students an opportunity to work with the protagonist, antagonist, and a selected minor character of a novel/library book.

2. Students must assess the characters by giving the **dominant impression** of each in terms of the most applicable adjectives that could be used to describe them.

3. Students then must do the following:

   a. Review and apply the six methods of characterization
   b. Cite examples from their novel to support each method
   c. Give internal documentation
   d. Give a complete bibliographic entry

4. **"What a Character!"** works well with a **persuasive writing unit** in that students are making a case for their character analyses to be accurate as supported by textual material.

Name:____________________ Class:________________ Date:______________

What a Character!

From your library book quote passages that will give a complete picture of the protagonist, antagonist, and a minor character.

I. Protagonist: Best adjective to describe the major character:____________________

➜ Support your choice by citing evidence for all methods of characterization. Be sure your choices relate to the adjective you've chosen and be sure that your quotations are typical of the character.

➜ Be sure to include internal footnotes.

A. Appearance:____

____

____

____

B. Speech:____

____

____

____

C. Actions: ______________________________
____
____
____

D. Inner thoughts and feelings: ______________________________
____
____
____

E. What others say: ______________________________
____
____
____

F. Environment: ______________________________
____
____
____

II. Antagonist: Best adjective to describe the adversary: ____________________

➜ Quote three incidents that prove that the antagonist is worthy of your description and explain.

A.

1. Incident: ______________________________
____
____

2. Explanation:______________________________

____

____

B.

1. Incident:______________________________

____

____

2. Explanation:______________________________

____

____

C.

1. Incident:______________________________

____

____

2. Explanation:______________________________

____

____

III. Minor Character: What do you think the author's purpose is to include this minor character in the plot?

____

____

➔ Quote two examples from the book and explain.

A.

1. Quote:____

2. Explanation:____________________________________

B.

1. Quote:____

2. Explanation:____________________________________

Bibliographic Entry:__________________________________

Name:________________Class:________Date:________

Books I Read THIS SEMESTER

1.________________________________

2.________________________________

3.________________________________

4.________________________________

5.________________________________

6.________________________________

7.________________________________

8.________________________________

9.________________________________

10.________________________________

PART II

NARRATIVE RESEARCH

How to Write a Narrative Research Paper

1. Students enjoy telling stories, and what better way to entice them to learn research skills than by requiring that the final product of their research unit be a narrative of their choice that **weaves researched, documented facts** into its story line.

2. Students should be prepared for their time spent in the **library** by doing the following activities:

   A. Each student should brainstorm a list of **ten possible story ideas.** The best stories seem to come from the student's own reality--or at least be "typical" stories that could be told by some of the student's own age group.

   B. The student should then draw a **"working" plot graph,** one that contains at least *five rising actions, one climax, and one falling action.* Of course, as the story takes shape, the graph may be revised.

   C. Each student should then graph a **working web** of ideas to be researched.

      1. The **central spoke** of the web should be the story line or the title of the story.

      2. Each of the **secondary circles** could be elements central to the story, *such as characterization, theme, etc.*

3. The **final circles** extending from these central elements should be **questions** that need to be researched. For instance, perhaps a student needs to look up information about a famous person to be mentioned in the story. Or maybe the student wants to include details about a setting or a historical fact. Again, the research web may change, but the initial web forces the student to brainstorm research ideas.

D. As a class, read a set of **"typical" stories**, from Sandra Cisneros' "Eleven" to Maureen Daly's "Sixteen."

E. Analyze **"Sixteen"** in terms of the elements of a short story and show students how Daly, had she not written the story during the time the story is set, would have had to have done **research** on various aspects of the story to make it accurate and believable (e.g., Stalin, Garbo, Winchell, etc.).

♡♡ A **Sample Analysis** is provided that highlights researched aspects of **"Sixteen"**

Name:______________________________ Class:____________ Date:________________

Analysis of Maureen Daly's "Sixteen"

1. Cite the reference made to a magazine article that speaks of Russian women.

____

____

____

2. A. In this quotation regarding the magazine article, what famous person is mentioned?

____

B. Look up the person and cite information that would help the reader better understand the setting of the story and use an internal footnote for documentation.

____

____

____

C. Give a bibliographic entry for your information.

____

____

____

ANALYSIS OF "SIXTEEN"

3. A. **On the first page of the story,** two other famous people **are mentioned. Quote the passages that refer to these people.**

1. ______________________________

____

2. ______________________________

____

B. Choose one person **and look up facts that would give needed** background information **regarding the story. Use an internal footnote to give attribution.**

____

____

____

C. **Write a** bibliographic entry.

____

____

____

4. A. **Quote passages that refer to** two other famous people.

1. ______________________________

____

2. ______________________________

____

B. Choose one **of the above to look up and explain how knowing this reference adds to a** reader's understanding **of the story. Use an internal footnote.**

____

____

____

5. **Quote a passage from the story** (other than passages already cited above) **that is a clue to the fact that the** setting **is not the present and explain your choice.**

A. Quote: ____

____

B. Explanation: ____

____

6. **In your own words, explain the** plot **of the story.** (Remember to tell the beginning, middle, and end--as in a summary.)

____

____

____

7. **Explain the** theme (the universal lesson learned) **of the story.**

____

____

____

ANALYSIS OF "SIXTEEN"

8. Quote five examples of the following figurative language devices:

A. Simile: ______________________________

____

B. Explicit Metaphor: ______________________________

____

C. Implicit Metaphor: ______________________________

____

D. Personification: ______________________________

____

E. Hyperbole: ______________________________

____

9. A. Quote a pathetic fallacy.

____

____

B. Explain its effect: ______________________________

____

____

10. Explain why this story could have a universal appeal.

____

____

____

Answers to:

Analysis of Maureen Daly's "Sixteen"

1. " 'And Stalin says the future of Russia lies in its women. In its women who have tilled its soil, raised its children--' "

2. A. Stalin
   B. Joseph Stalin--1879-1953--Russian statesman, secretary general of the Communist party 1922-53 (Stein, ed. 1384)
   C. Stein, Jess, ed. The Random House Dictionary. New York: Random House, 1966.

3. A. 1. "I read Walter Winchell's column. You get to know what New York boy is that way about some pineapple princess on the West Coast and what Paradise pretty is currently the prettiest...."
   2. "...and why someone, eventually will play Scarlett O'Hara."

   B. Walter Winchell (1897-1972)--radio personality; newspaper columnist; 15-minute broadcasts on Sunday nights (1932-1950's); "He had a knack for digging out personal details about show business figures and cafe society" ("Walter Winchell" n.p.).

   C. "Walter Winchell," Compton's Interactive Encyclopedia, 1994.

4. A. 1. " 'Black ones,' I told him. 'Same size as Garbo's.' "
   2. "A very respectable Emily Post sort of conversation...."

   B. Knowing that Greta Garbo was a "haunting beauty" and that her "success was spectacular and her popularity enormous," the reader can better understand why the narrator tells her new friend that her shoes are the same size as Garbo's. She is aggrandizing herself, making herself seem more sophisticated by likening herself in some way--albeit the shoe size--to such a famous star ("Greta Garbo" n.p.).

ANALYSIS OF "SIXTEEN"

5. **A.** "And I know that anyone who orders a strawberry sundae in a drugstore instead of a lemon coke would probably be dumb enough to...wear Evening in Paris with a tweed suit."

B. Present-day "drugstores" don't have soda fountains or offer "lemon cokes," and Evening in Paris is a perfume of the "past."

6. A supposedly sophisticated girl, who "gets around," meets a boy at a skating rink, has a good time, and is falsely led to believe that he'll call for another "date." (Answers will vary.)

7. People's words aren't always good. (Answers will vary.)

8. Answers will vary.

A. "The ashes crunched like crackerjack...."

B. "The night was an etching in black and white."

C. "She panted along beside me and her hot breath made a frosty little balloon balancing on the end of her nose."

D. "...and the stars winked down...."

E. "Outside the night is still, so still I think I'll go crazy...."

9. **A.** "I shivered. Somehow the darkness seemed changed. The stars were little hard chips of light far up in the sky and the moon stared down with a sullen yellow glare."

B. The effect is that the reader realizes that all the "loveliness" that the narrator had felt when she had hope turns suddenly into "harsh" reality, thus environment mirroring a character's feelings.

10. The story could have universal appeal in that its theme of rejection/lies/false intentions is a common one with which most people can identify, and its plot is typical as well. Most of us have had a special time that for some reason is not able to be repeated. Besides the theme and plot, the specific details make the story come alive for the readers. We can see the "pimply-faced boy grabb(ing) the hat from the frizzled head of an eighth-grade blonde," and we can feel the narrator's anguish as she sits there, not "feeling anything."

Narrative Research Syllabuses
Two Variations

1. The first syllabus--**Syllabus for Narrative Research Paper**--is designed for a **two-week library unit involving a 45-minute class session.** The same lesson can be done, however, during a 90-minute block period.

   A. This assignment results in a narrative with documented facts. The **length** of the final paper, as well as the **number of note cards actually used** in the final draft, is at the teacher's discretion; however, most stories run **3-5 typed pages** and use at least **10 facts** from note cards.

   B. Each day's **lesson plans** are mapped out for the teacher's, students', and librarian's use.

      1. The **First Day** concentrates on the **year of the story's setting** and requires **five note cards of events** that occur during that year, besides the sample note cards for each source type that students can use for reference throughout their library time.

      2. The **Third Day** focuses on sensory images of **sight** and requires **five cards.**

3. **Day Four** asks for **five cards** regarding **famous people** that could be included in the story.

4. **Day Six's** requirements are **five facts** about a **topic** of the story while **Day Seven** calls for another **five cards** on **sensory images,** besides those of sight.

5. **Day Eight's** lesson centers on **themes** that could be revealed through **famous quotations,** thus teaching or reinforcing students' use of quotation books/Internet.

2. The second syllabus--**Syllabus for Alphabet Narrative Research Paper**--is different in that students must have at least **twenty-six note cards,** one for every letter of the alphabet (e.g., Alaska=a possible setting; baseball=a possible plot idea or topic; Cronkite=a famous person). Students enjoy the "game" of figuring how to include facts from as many of their alphabet letter note cards as possible. Extra credit can be given to students who use all twenty-six.

3. Whichever syllabus is used, students, parents, librarians, and administrators **appreciate an organized syllabus.** Students who find it necessary to be absent some time during the unit have a ready-made assignment sheet to follow on their return.

Name:______________________ Class:______________ Date:__________

Syllabus for Narrative Research Paper

Day One--Orientation

1. Take a **sample note card** for books, encyclopedias, and magazines.
2. From your list of **brainstormed story ideas**, choose a story that you would like to tell.
3. Determine the **time frame** of the story--the **year** of the setting.
4. Begin taking **five note cards** for events that occurred during the year your story takes place.

⇨ *If your story takes place in the year 1990, research five events that happened during that time period. Some of these might become **background information** that you would mention in your story to make the setting more believable for your reader.*

Day Two--Story/Events

1. Read "Sixteen" by Maureen Daly as an example of a narrative.

2. Finish events note cards.

Day Three--Sight note cards

1. Brainstorm/web five possible researchable sights you could "see" from the setting of your story.

2. Begin taking five note cards for the sense of sight, describing through research specific things you could see from your setting.

⇨ You could research one sight and take five note cards about it, or you could research five different sights and take one note card about each.

⇨ If your story is about your dance camp experience in Marshall, Texas, you might want to research specific lakes that could serve as a realistic setting for the camp as well as names of nearby towns that could be mentioned somewhere in your story.

Day Four--Famous people

1. Brainstorm/web five famous people you might want to mention in your story.

2. Begin taking five note cards on one or more of these people.

⇨ In the dance camp story, you might want to include a passing reference to a famous dancer or choreographer.

Day Five--Catch-up Day

1. **Catch up** on any of the types of note cards taken so far this week.
2. If you are already caught up, you may do more of any type studied so far for **extra credit.**

Day Six--Facts about your topic

1. Brainstorm\web **five facts about your topic** that you might need to include in your story.
2. Begin taking **five note cards** about one or more of these facts.

⇨ In the dance camp story, you might want to include the French names of specific dance steps to add authenticity to your story.

Day Seven--Second sense day

1. **Brainstorm/web another sense** or a combination of senses that you could include in the descriptive aspect of your story.
2. Begin taking **five note cards** on one or more sense images.

⇨ Smells could include certain flowers of a region or specific chemical emissions.

⇨ Tastes could include specific information about certain exotic food.

Day Eight--Theme/quotation day

1. Brainstorm/web a possible **theme** for your story (i.e., a lesson the reader could learn).

2. Begin taking **five note cards** on themes that could fit your story.

⇨ For "One July Long Ago," the reader learns that life can take a turn for the better.

3. If you are unsure as to the theme that you might be working toward, you may look up **famous sayings** that you might want to include in your story. Be sure to avoid CLICHÉS (overused statements).

Days Nine and Ten--Catch-up days

1. **Catch up** on any note cards not completed during the week.

2. If you are caught up, you may take any extra note cards for **extra credit.**

Name:______________________ Class:____________________ Date:__________

Syllabus for Alphabet Narrative Research Paper

Product: **A narrative vignette** (3-5 pages typed, double-spaced, whose time frame is one day maximum, preferably shorter).

Model: **Maureen Daly's "Sixteen"** (written when the author was sixteen: Daly was the first high school student to have a story included in the O'Henry Memorial Award Prize Stories).

Assignment:

1. **Expanded moment**--**You will be required to concentrate on moments, giving details, examining what is done, said, thought about in a short period of time. Senses will be used to heighten the effect.**

2. **Elements of a short story**--**You will identify the following basic elements as you have created them in your writing:**

   A. Setting
   B. Characterization
   C. Conflict
   D. Plot--rising action, climax, falling action
   E. Tone/Mood
   F. Theme
   G. Point of view

3. Reading Objectives: Besides the elements listed above, you will apply the following reading objectives to your story:

A. Cause/Effect
B. Inference
C. Fact/Opinion
D. Summarization
E. Prediction

4. Figurative Language/Stylistic Devices--You will include and label at least one example of each of the following devices:

A. Repetition for effect
B. Simile
C. Metaphor
D. Personification
E. Hyperbole
F. Internal Monologue

Research Requirements:

1. Twenty-six note cards representing one fact for every letter of the alphabet:

*A=Alaska (a possible setting)
*B=Baseball (a possible plot idea)
*C=Cronkite (a possible famous person)

A. Each card will include one thought summarized in your own words.

B. Material should be **quoted** only when the wording is so eloquent that to summarize would be to lessen the effect or when the source or the wording itself could add "persuasive punch" to your work.

C. Each card will be labeled in the **top right corner** with a letter that corresponds to the letter of the source card and with the page number where the information was found.

2. Appropriate **bibliographic cards** for each note card:

A. The form will be that of the **MLA.**

B. Each bibliographic card will be labeled with a letter that corresponds to the appropriate note card.

3. The **subjects of the note cards** should include at least the following:

A. **Setting**

1. **Time** (e.g.., information concerning the 1960's)
2. **Place** (e.g., a town, a state, wild flowers indigenous to the region)

B. **Character** (e.g., perhaps a famous person you could allude to as Maureen Daly does with Greta Garbo in "Sixteen")

C. **Plot** (e.g., "Sixteen" could have mentioned skating terminology. Benny and Joon was based on the disease schizophrenia. What facts could you mention concerning your plot?)

D. **Conflict--A dialogue between two characters could involve researched facts, and/or your internal monologue could reveal facts,** such as in "Sixteen" when the narrator sets the stage using Walter Winchell, Stalin, Scarlet O'Hara--all signs of the times, all researchable facts.

4. Sources **must include at least one example from each of the following:**

A. Book
B. Encyclopedia
C. Magazine
D. Atlas
E. Almanac
F. Contemporary Authors
G. Quotation Book
H. Newspaper
I. Internet
J. Special Dictionary

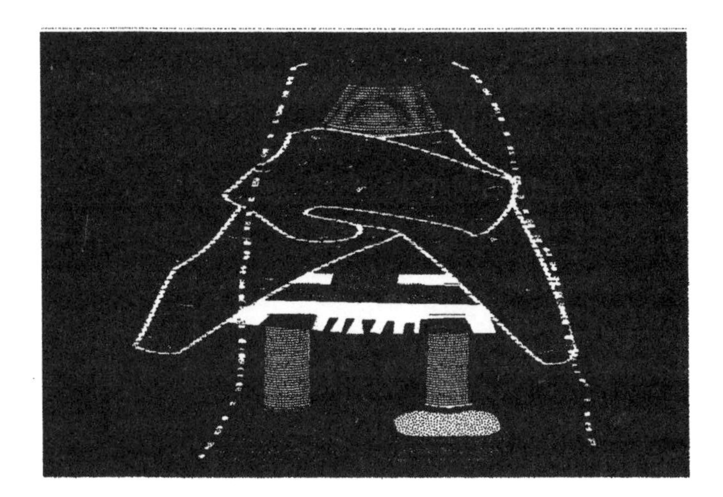

5. Periodic Checks **will be made on note cards, bibliographic cards, and story ideas** (i.e., web. Plot graph, rough drafts, etc.).

6. For the actual story, a minimum of ten internal footnotes will be used.

How to Use Rubrics

1. **Rubrics** are designed to do the following:

   a. To serve as **guidelines for what is expected** in a final product, including **points on which a grade can be based.**

   b. To provide students with a **structural picture** of an excellent paper.

   c. To provide an **organized approach to revision**, which is the key to a student writer's growth.

2. **Rubrics** may be used in the following ways:

   a. Hand out rubrics **after the initial rough drafts are completed** since rubrics **can signal errors in structure**--which necessitate deep revisionary strategies--as well as in **mechanics**, which could simply be a stage in the final proofreading.

   b. Instruct students to **complete every aspect of the rubric**, leaving no part incomplete. For example, if the rubric calls for five figurative language devices, the point is not for the student to include the two his or her paper currently contains and think that satisfies the requirement but to **revise the paper accordingly** to include three extra devices.

3. Rubrics may be graded in the following manners:

a. Rubrics can be **spot-checked for effort and given a nominal grade.** If a class has worked on **certain skills** (e.g., run-ons and fragments), only the section of the rubric dealing with those lessons may be graded.

Or

b. Rubrics can be handed in and **graded before the final draft of the paper,** serving as a sort of **outline of the necessary components,** and checked by the teacher in much the same way as rough drafts are often reviewed. Or

c. One effective method is to **grade rubrics on how successful each aspect was in terms of producing a better product.** For instance, if no errors in organization occurred in the final draft of the paper itself, no points would be deducted from the rubric for that section. If, however, mechanical errors such as run-ons or fragments detracted from the value of the paper, a designated number of points could be subtracted, indicating to the writer that more time needs to be spent proofreading for these sorts of errors.

d. Rubrics can be used as **oral-conference grades**--the student and teacher together focusing on problem areas, strengths, etc.

NAME______________________ CLASS____________ DATE____________

Rubric #1
Research Narrative Vignette

Label the following **literary elements** in your narrative vignette and **quote an example** for each from your paper in order to prove its inclusion.

1. Setting--time and place

____

____

2. Point of view--Circle: first person, third person, or omniscient

____

____

3. Tone/Mood--

a. Tone=Author's attitude toward his/her subject

____

____

B. Mood=reader's response toward the work

____

____

4. Conflict--(problem; struggle of opposing forces)

Circle the main type: internal or external

____

____

5. Characterization--For your major character, choose which two methods of characterization you rely on the most and give an example for each:

✏ *Methods:* appearance, environment, inner thoughts and feelings, actions, speech, what others say

a. ____

____

b. ____

____

6. Plot--rising action, climax, falling action

a. Rising action--Label at least **five major points** of rising action in your story. List the **first one** below:

____

b. Climax--

c. Falling Action--

7. Theme--main idea; universal lesson learned (stated or implied)

Name:____________________________**Class:**______________**Date:**________________

Rubric #2

Research Narrative Vignette

Label the following literary elements in your narrative vignette and quote an example for each from your research paper in order to prove its inclusion.

1. A. Repetition for effect:____________________________

____

____

B. Explain the effect you are trying to create:__________________

____

____

2. A. Simile (Be sure to quote both elements being compared.):

____

____

____

B. Explain how this is an **effective simile:** ____________________

____

3. A. Metaphor: ____________________

____

____

B. Is this an **explicit metaphor** (one that usually has a "be" verb and states both elements being compared--e.g., She was a robot.) or an **implicit metaphor** (one that implies a comparison--e.g., the blackberry sky)?

____

4. A. Personification: ____________________

____

____

B. What is the **human trait** you are attributing to an inanimate object or to an abstraction?

____

5. A. Hyperbole: ____________________

____

____

B. Explain **how** this is an **exaggeration for effect:**

____

____

Rubric #2

6. A. Internal Monologue: ____________________

____

____

____

B. How is this an effective internal monologue?

____

____

____

7. A. Expanded Moment: ____________________

____

____

____

____

B. What is the effect of this expanded moment?

____

____

____

NAME:________________________ CLASS:________________________ DATE:________________

RUBRIC #3
RESEARCH NARRATIVE VIGNETTE

Label the following **READING/LITERARY ELEMENTS** in your narrative vignette and **QUOTE** an example for each from your paper in order to prove its inclusion.

1. **INTERNAL FOOTNOTE**--Give a sentence that contains a **FACT** and show your **DOCUMENTATION**.

____

____

____

2. **PREDICTION**-- Quote a part of your story that would cause readers to make a prediction and explain what the reader might predict.

A. **QUOTE:** ____

B. **EXPLANATION:** ____

____

3. **FACT/OPINION**--Give a **DIFFERENT FACT** from question #1 and contrast it with an opinion from your story.

A. **FACT:** ____

B. **OPINION:** ______________________________

____

4. **CAUSE/EFFECT**--Quote a cause/effect relationship in your story. If quoting is impossible, explain the relationship.

A. **CAUSE:** ______________________________

____

B. **EFFECT:** ______________________________

____

5. **INFERENCE**--Quote a passage where a reader could infer something and explain the inference.

A. **QUOTE:** ______________________________

____

B. **EXPLANATION:** ______________________________

____

6. **SUMMARIZATION**--Pretend your story is a movie of the week for television. Write a summary that could appear in **TV GUIDE**.

____

____

Name:____________________ Class:____________________________ Date:____________________

RUBRIC #4
RESEARCH NARRATIVE VIGNETTE
PART 1

PUNCTUATE the following ***SAMPLE SENTENCES*** from narrative research papers. On the lines below, **TELL THE *RULE*(s).**

1. "Daddy why are you making me do this? You know I don't want to go to camp!"

   RULE: ____

2. I didn't want to go but they made me.

   RULE: ____

3. It was like the army I was a private they were colonels.

   RULE: ____

4. Or generals. (Here you have to rewrite the "sentence".)

   REWRITE: ____

   RULE: ____

5. My mother the dictator told me how much I'd love the experience.

   RULE: ____

6. I'm Robert Joffrey he said to me. I'm Pettie Rollo I answered, amazed that finally I was able to meet my hero.

   ✏ Here you have to rewrite the sentence, using **QUOTATION *MARKS*** and starting a ***NEW PARAGRAPH*** for each new speaker. The rule will be a comma rule.

Rubric #4

REWRITE:--

RULE: ____

7. Well that was like a home run an orbit around Earth or a Nobel Prize. (Three commas, two rules)

   RULES: ____________________ & ____________________

8. I didn't want him to know I was from Baytown Texas at least not yet.

   RULE: ____

PART 2

FROM YOUR RESEARCH PAPER, copy 5 sentences that exemplify **VARIOUS COMMA RULES**. Circle the commas and on the lines below, tell the rules.

#1. SENTENCE: ____

____

RULE: ____

#2. SENTENCE: ____

____

RULE: ____

#3. SENTENCE: ____

____

RULE: ________________________________

#4. SENTENCE: ________________________________

____

RULE: ________________________________

#5. SENTENCE: ________________________________

____

RULE: ________________________________

PART 3

USING YOUR RESEARCH PAPER, copy 2 examples of sentences that exemplify other grammar rules **BESIDES COMMAS, END PUNCTUATION, AND QUOTATION MARKS.** You could choose adjective/adverb usage, pronoun case, or subject/verb agreement.

#1. SENTENCE: ________________________________

____

RULE: ________________________________

#2. SENTENCE: ________________________________

____

RULE: ________________________________

Answers to:

Rubric #4
Research Narrative Vignette

1. **Direct Address:** Daddy,
2. **Compound Sentence:** go,
3. **Run-Ons:** army; I was a private, and they were colonels.
4. **Fragment:** They were colonels or generals. **(Answers will vary.)**
5. **Appositive:** mother, dictator,
6. **Direct Quotation:**

   "I'm Robert Joffrey," he said to me.
   "I'm Pettie Rollo," I answered....

7. **Introductory Word:** Well,
   Series: run, Earth,
8. **Address:** Baytown, Texas,

Name:_________________________Class:_______________Date:_______________

Rubric #5
Research Narrative Vignette

To review **punctuation skills** for your research paper, punctuate the following sentences from "One July Long Ago" and "Today I Will Remember" and give the appropriate rule(s) on the lines to the left of the numbers.

____________________**1.** I was twelve and my summer plans were fizzling like the Bay of Pigs Invasion.

____________________**2.** You're going and that's that young lady Daddy had said his voice stern his face muscles tight his eyes narrowed....

____________________**3.** Did I know they had chirped that Steinbeck had finished The Winter of Our Discontent and that farthings were no longer legal tender in Britain and that New York defeated Cincinnati in the World Series?

____________________**4.** All I could do was daydream about Mike my boyfriend.

____________________**5.** Well no movies yet but we did talk a lot about Billy Palmer the fat boy and Arthur Appleton the math whiz and food fights in the cafeteria....

____________________**6.** Robert Joffrey who choreographed ballets for the American Ballet Theater....

____________________**7.** The 1960s was a decade of firsts the first Catholic elected President the first black selected NBA coach the first time three fourths of a TV viewing nation watched the Beatles on The Ed Sullivan Show and the first time Id hear old lady Ginsburgs raspy voice over my junior high school auditoriums microphone.

____________________**8.** Okay students empty seats between each of you.

Rubric #5: Narrative Vignette Research Paper

____________________ **9.** If a bushel of wheat makes 315 loaves of bread each weighing one pound two ounces how many loaves of this weight can be made with 473 bushels of wheat?

____________________ **10.** Today Ill sit an empty seat to each side of me listening to the almost inaudible sound of Mrs. Ginsburgs rubber soled shoes.

To review other **grammatical rules**, correct the following excerpts from the same research papers and give the rule(s) that apply.

____________________ **1.** People in the third row, Mr. Biddle's class, you need to file in quiet.

____________________ **2.** Something you hadn't planned on.

____________________ **3.** So, boys and girls, you know the rules, each section of the eight-section test is timed....

____________________ **4.** Maybe I'll be asked to explain Transcendentalism in 25 words or less.

____________________ **5.** What kind of place is this to determine our future based solely on memorization of facts from a past us kids didn't create?

____________________ **6.** It was fast becoming my experience that fiascos and walls is not limited to the political.

____________________ **7.** I had hummed every song from are you lonesome tonight to will you love me tonight to tossin' and turnin'.

____________________ **8.** It was as if he was bracing himself for another session of preteen whining.

____________________ **9.** That had been it, the last words the two generations had spoke.

____________________ **10.** I had threw myself into the part like Elizabeth Taylor in Cleopatra

a.

Answers to:

Rubric #5
Research Narrative Vignette

1.	**Compound Sentence:**	twelve,
2.	**Compound Sentence:** **Direct Address:** **Direct Quotation:** **Series:**	"You're going, and that's that, young lady," Daddy had said, his voice stern, his face muscles tight, his eyes....
3.	**Direct Quotation:** **Book Title:**	"Did I know," they had chirped, "that Steinbeck had finished The Winter of Our Discontent... Series?"
4.	**Appositive:**	Mike,
5.	**Introductory Word:** **Compound Sentence:** **Appositive:**	Well, yet, Palmer,...boy, Arthur Appleton...whiz,
6.	**Non-Restrictive Clause:**	Joffrey,
7.	**Colon for lists:** **Series:** **TV show:** **Apostrophes:**	firsts: President, coach, "Ed Sullivan Show" I'd Ginsburg's auditorium's
8.	**Direct Address:**	Okay, students,
9.	**Introductory Adverb Clause:**	ounces,
10.	**Apostrophe:** **Interrupters:** **Apostrophe:** **Hyphenated Adjective:**	I'll sit, ...me, Ginsburg's rubber-soled

Answers to:

Grammatical Rules

1. **Adverb Usage:** quietly
2. **Fragment:** Something you hadn't planned on happened. **(Answers will vary.)**
3. **Run-On:** rules; **(or another way to correct a run-on)**
4. **Less/Fewer:** fewer
5. **Pronoun Case:** we
6. **Subject/Verb Agreement:** are
7. **Song Titles:** "Are You Lonesome Tonight?" "Will You Love Me Tonight?" "Tossin' and Turnin'"
8. **Subjunctive Mood:** were
9. **Verb Form:** spoken
10. **Verb Form:** thrown
    Movie Title: Cleopatra

NAME:______________________ **CLASS:**________________ **DATE:**__________

Final Check Sheet for Research Paper

The following papers should be in your final packet in this order:

_____1. **Decorative cover**--picture(s) illustrating your narrative

_____2. **Title page**--title of narrative in center; full heading in lower right corner

_____3. **Table of Contents**--list of contents of your packet by page number

_____4. **Final plot graph**--final plot graph using different colors to denote rising actions, climax, and falling action

_____5. **Final web** of researched material--final copy of web illustrating where researched material is placed (e.g., setting: Marshall, Texas--note cards on the town itself)

_____6. **Chart/Graph**--extra credit chart or graph illustrating an aspect of your paper; remember to footnote your source at the bottom of your graph in a bibliographic entry.

_____7. **Final paper**--TWO COPIES OF THE FINAL PAPER are necessary: one for you to read to the class while your peers evaluate you on various teacher-assigned aspects; the other for your teacher to correct and mark questions for the class as you read

_____a. All internal footnotes must be colored on both copies. A separate color must be used for each source.

_____b. All literary elements/stylistic devices

of the narrative must be labeled in the margin. See assignment sheet.

_______ c. Signature of parent on final draft

_____ 8. **Final copy of bibliography**--Remember to have only those entries whose source cards were used. Don't forget to do the following:

_____ a. Alphabetize.

_____ b. Indent all lines except first line of each entry.

_____ c. Don't number entries.

_____ d. Do follow each mark of punctuation carefully, including the period at the end of each entry.

______ 9. Note cards used as **footnotes** in your paper--

_____ a. Note cards that were actually used as footnotes in your paper must be colored to match the footnote of your paper.

_____ b. These note cards must be stapled separately to a sheet of typing paper for easy reference.

_____ c. Include a legend note card, which is a color-coded listing of the number of footnotes for each category (corresponding to your webbing categories) and the total number used for the paper.

______ 10. All **rough drafts** of your research paper

______ 11. All **rubrics**

✔ **Final due date** of project is ______________________.

✔ **Extras** used to enhance presentation: ______________________.

"One July Long Ago"
Teacher as Writer/Participant

1. **In an effort to be true to the** writing process, **to view all members of the class--including the teacher--as active participants in the writing community, the teacher should make an effort to** participate in all stages of the writing process with his/her students.

2. "One July Long Ago" **is an effort to share with students a** typical, true-to-life story **made more believable and more interesting with the addition of** researched facts.

Teacher Model
Narrative Research Paper

One July Long Ago

It was 1961. Only one year had passed since John F. Kennedy's inspirational inaugural address. The "New Frontier" of Americans, the "new generation," he had called us, as he spurred us on to victory. We would personally succeed, he had implied, when our country succeeded. We must, this brave new leader told us, "'Ask not what your country can do for you, but what you can do for your country'" (Emmens 2-3). We were to remember 1961 as a year of promise. Roger Maris scored sixty-one homeruns, Mickey Mantle fifty-four (Emmens 79). The first man orbited the Earth in less than two hours (Emmens 35). M. Calvin won the Nobel Prize for chemistry for his work with photosynthesis (Grun 549). It was unarguably a time of great men doing great things. But victory and success and greatness weren't in the cards for me that year. I was twelve, and my summer plans were fizzling like the Bay of Pigs invasion. Twelve hundred Cuban exiles couldn't

defeat Castro ("Bay of Pigs Invasion" 893) and I was learning fast that one twelve-year-old didn't stand a chance on the home front, at least not when my t.v., telephone, and curfew were controlled by the old frontier, the old generation, my parents.

"You're going, and that's that, young lady!" Daddy had said, his voice stern, his face muscles tight, his eyes narrowed, as if he were bracing himself for another grueling session of preteen whining.

And I hadn't disappointed him. "Daddy," I had sniffed, I had puckered, I had pleaded, throwing myself into the part like Elizabeth Taylor in <u>Cleopatra</u>. "I don't want to go. I'll be miserable. How will I ever survive without you and Mama?" I had cried, dabbing my eyes, blowing my nose, and generally looking as if I had caught a twenty-four-hour something-or-other, or at least hoping I had.

"You'll make it fine, dear. Just like all the other girls."

"What was happening to my life?" I had thought as the next two weeks flashed before my eyes like the one-horse Texas towns we would pass on the way to Marshall. Dayton, Liberty, Hardin, Livingston (Exxon map)--I was doomed. Rusk, Alto, Lufkin, Henderson (Exxon map)--How would I make it?

But that had been it, the last words the two generations had spoken before we drove up the long gravel road to Camp Tawanda that hot, muggy day in July. I had spent the three-hour ride doing what all twelve-year-old girls do. I had hummed

every song from "Are You Lonesome Tonight" to "Will You Love Me Tonight" to "Tossin' and Turn'" (Grun 74). I had ignored my parents' brilliant front-seat conversation. Did I know, they had chirped, that Steinbeck had finished The Winter of Our Discontent (Grun 549) and that farthings were no longer legal tender in Britain (Grun 549) and that New York defeated Cincinnati in the World Series (Grun 549)?

Did I know? Did I care was more to the point. I couldn't think about books or farthings or baseball. All I could do was daydream about Mike, my boyfriend. Oh, we hadn't actually gone on a date or anything. Mama had said it would be over her dead body, and Daddy had gotten all stern-voiced again and puffy in the face like he was going to blow a gasket or something when I even mentioned that maybe sometime somebody could drive us to the movies or something.

Well, no movies yet, but we did talk a lot about Billy Palmer, the fat boy, and Arthur Appleton, the math whiz, and food fights in the school cafeteria and whether or not my mother would send Mike's favorite--ripe red strawberries to be dipped in fine granulated sugar she'd pack in folded wax paper next to my meat loaf sandwich. And I had just been up to wondering if Mrs. Ginsburg's walleye was real or not when Mama chimed in with "Longview! We're almost there, sweetie."

So Billy Palmer, Arthur Appleton, junior high cafeterias, and strawberries dipped in sugar were put on hold for a while. Our

Buick LeSabre pulled up in front of a cluster of rustic cabins smack dab in the middle of the densest woods I had ever seen. It would have been like a setting for a horror movie if it hadn't been for the break in the thicket that led to a fantastic, and at least on my part, unexpected view of Caddo Lake. All of a sudden there was all this water, like a blue jewel in the midst of black velvet. Of course, it took us forever to come to a full stop, what with Daddy driving like he was a year older than Methuselah and Mama cataloguing every species of flower known to man. "Look, everyone, an *Anemone blanda* (Druse 139). And over there a *Begonia semperflorens* (Druse 139)."

My parents always knew what they were talking about, I'll give them that, but I don't know--sometimes I wish they were stupid. Or wrong. Or something. It was embarrassing. It was like they had all this love, all these expectations, all for me. And what had I ever done except learn to ride a bicycle without hands--well, almost--or to hold on, without falling off once, the whole way from the top of the hill down to the bayou on Claudia's backyard trolley swing, or to take ballet lessons? I guess that's why Daddy was always calling me his little ballerina. What else could he call me? His little bicycle rider, his little trolley swinger? And Mother, her hopes were so high for me that I'd have to live to be ninety to get in all the stuff she expected.

"This will be good for you, baby," she had said all spring and into the summer. It would, to hear her tell it, quote/unquote provide me with an aesthetic experience.

Well, all it had provided me with so far was one sprung rump, one headache the size of "Big-D-double-l-a-s," and enough scientific data about plants to write a doctoral dissertation on the subject. I could just see these two weeks now--me and the *Impatiens wallerina* (Druse 139), me and the two-ton bear that would probably crush my skull as I make my way to breakfasts of runny eggs and greasy bacon, me and 100 other dopey kids. Me and a fat, bald teacher old enough to be my grandfather. Me and....

And then I saw him. I no sooner set foot on Marshall terrain, a *Phlox adsurgens* to the right of me, a lungwort (Druse 139) to the left, both of which--thanks to Mother--I recognized as perennials indigenous to shady southern terrain (Druse 139), no sooner gotten myself unwound from backseat riding like some doughy pretzel finally pulled apart, no sooner started in on the whining, one final session to let them know my anguish, to insure that their two weeks without me would be far from guilt-free, no sooner had I done all this than life as I had known it changed.

My parents' chattering and chirping about the accommodations fell on deaf ears. Their admonitions that my stay be an edifying one became no more than background music that wafted up and over the treetops. Mike, thoughts of Mike, were as distant and far removed as the gift Aunt Bertha had given me for Christmas. Who was Aunt Bertha anyway? And Mike who? All I knew was that I had seen him--every girl's dream, the embodiment, the essence of dance itself--Robert. Robert Joffrey. I had seen his

ballet le Bal Masque, "a symbolic interpretation of man's blindness to reality" (Gadan 190), the program had said, and I had seen the man himself through binoculars from the balcony at the Music Hall, but this, I had no idea I would be seeing the legend in person.

And then it happened.

He extended his hand in a continental greeting, as if he were about to raise my fingers to his lips or to help me like a gallant gentleman of old up to a waiting carriage or to ever so securely guide me across a crowded street. And if this unprecedented gesture weren't enough, he asked if he could carry my luggage, taking the bulging pieces from Father, one worldly, wise, experienced man assisting another.

But more than that, he turned to me. Robert Joffrey, who choreographed ballets for the American Ballet Theater, who was a former student of Alexandra Fedorova (Gadan 190), Robert Joffrey turned to me and said he looked forward to having me, I Rollo, in class.

And to my twelve-year-old psyche that meant all the world. It was a home run, an orbit around Earth, a Nobel Prize. It was a victory of sorts, a promise. And it was mine alone.

Whatever else happened those two weeks one July long, long ago, one thing is certain--President Kennedy had been right. I was the new generation, and I had my whole life ahead of me.

Teacher Model
Narrative Research Paper

Today I Will Remember

The 1960's was a decade of firsts: the first Catholic elected President ("Kennedy Family" 759), the first black selected NBA coach (Emmens 82), the first time three-fourths of a TV-viewing nation watched the Beatles on " The Ed Sullivan Show" (Emmens 60), and...the first time I'd hear old lady Ginsburg's raspy voice over my junior high school auditorium's microphone.

The Bay of Pigs invasion was deemed a "fiasco" (Emmens 7), East and West Berlin were now separated by a wall ("Berlin" 1003), Nixon's campaign slogan was, prophetically, "Experience counts" (Emmens 3), and...well, it was fast becoming my experience that fiascos and walls are not limited to the political....

"Okay, students, empty seats between each of you! Empty seats, students, empty seats! Mrs. Riley's class, separate! No one should be sitting together. No sitting together! You know the rules, boys and girls. People in the third row, Mr. Biddle's class, you need to file in quietly. Quietly and quickly! We're about ready to begin. There's room for you over there--fifth and sixth rows behind Mrs. Swit's class.

Quickly, students, quickly!

"Now, classes, as you know, you'll be taking your National Assessment Test today, and I cannot stress, students, how important these scores are. They'll follow you wherever you go. They'll be on file in our junior high office and will travel with you to high school and then on to college and then on to the work force. Employers--and I hope you understand the import of this, students--your future employers will check these very credentials--the credentials you create today--when you seek employment so do not--repeat, do not--underestimate the effect of this test today, your seventh-grade year at D.J.H.S. What you do today, students, will stay with you always.

"So, boys and girls, you know the rules. Each section of the eight-section test is timed, approximately forty-five minutes per section, approximately 105 questions per time period, approximately two minutes between each section to regroup your forces. Any questions left unfinished will be marked incorrect. Any person suspected of cheating will be removed by our proctors. When you have finished a section, place your pencil to the right-hand side of your test and turn your test face down. Are there any questions, students before we begin?"

Are there any questions before we begin? Yeah, I think to myself, I've got one. I've got several, in fact. Like, hey Ginsburg, what if I need something simple during the test? Something you hadn't planned on. Something besides another pencil. Something more like a complete overhaul of my brain, like a trade-in for a brand-new model, or maybe just a lobotomy so I won't know the difference. Or, Ginsburg, got any ideas on a creative way to exit this joint, this auditorium filled with 357 kids?

Okay, 356. Kathy Cross is absent again today. Okay, maybe 340 or so. If Kathy's absent from our class and there are eleven classes of seventh graders, the law of averages might mean only 346 will see me swing from the rafters! Make that 343. I forgot about those three P.E. boys caught smoking in the bathroom last Friday.

And one last question, Ginsburg, how soon can mental illness be detected after its inception? Okay, maybe one more last question. Does mental illness have an inception? Great, I'm such the comic, such the math whiz. Pi? Yes, pi is exactly equal to the ratio 256/81 (Beckman preface). Tip-of-the-tongue stuff. Tiptop shape I am. Top of the morning to you, you old cretin.

Oh God, Mrs. Ginsburg, Mr. Biddle, everyone. L-E-T M-E O-U-T O-F H-E-R-E!

As I move only my eyes, my head riveted front, my entire body fearful of old lady Ginsburg approaching my left side, walking ever so slyly in her infamous rubber-soled Red Cross shoes, I can see--to the left of me, to the right of me, and straight ahead--that I am doomed. What kind of creativity can be born in such a sterile environment?

How's that question, Mrs. G.?

What kind of place is this to figure high-speed math? "If a bushel of wheat makes 315 loaves of bread each weighing one pound two ounces, how many loaves of this weight can be made with 473 bushels of wheat?" (Meyers 44) Right. Your typical man-on-the-street question. I'll just throw up a few fingers, crunch a few numbers, move a few digits, and presto! 148,995 loaves will drop via the heavens right onto the old answer sheet in 12 seconds flat. Let's see, that'll leave 44 minutes, 48 seconds for the rest of the 9,000 questions. I should be okay, yep, I should be okay.

Unless they drop a little Emersonian doctrine on me. Something maybe like explaining Transcendentalism--in 25 words or less. Or is it 25 words or fewer? Geez! a grammatical concept to consider mid-philosophizing. No problem. As if enlightened by Emerson and Carlyle and the whole intellectual circle of the 1830's New England (Pooley 247), as if I have only to light a cigarette, sip a glass of wine, and spew forth intuitively, I'll explain that transcendentalism is knowing the truth intuitively (Pooley 248), and I'll smile and go on to question #248. No problem. None whatsoever. None what...

What kind of place is this to determine our future based solely on memorization of facts from a past we didn't create?

Even my limited peripheral vision affords me row upon row of children, faces obediently front, bodies slumped in defeat, and hands nervously playing with pencils--that will ultimately be placed to the right of our face-down tests--or hopelessly, aimlessly, misleadingly at ease on desks that will soon hold papers that will soon hold our individual verdicts.

I can see Ryan Regan's progress already. Veritable hours before my completion he'll be done--finito, completo--his "A" as certain as old age and taxes. And Bob Palmer--whoever said Mama's boys finish last? This kid will be a National Merit scholar, Phi Beta Kappa, Fulbright, Rhodes, and God knows what else without even breathing hard.

And then there's me, my legs twisted around each other, my nails gnawed to a nub, my hands clammy--with forehead and underarms to match--trying unsuccessfully to figure where I was when God passed out instant recall.

There's so much injustice to this system. There's so much I know that I won't be able to express today. But today I will remember T.S.Eliot's "Four Quartet's": "We shall not cease from exploration..." (Plotz 6). Oh, and I won't. I'll explore and I'll learn and I'll remember. In time. My own time. And that desire, that drive, that will be what follows me the rest of my life.

Today? Today I'll sit, an empty seat to each side of me, listening to the almost inaudible sound of Mrs. Ginsburg's rubber-soled shoes.

Chad Morris
Research Narrative
Published in Merlyn's Pen

Passing Time

The month of June, 1986: a time that a friend tried to imitate ***LUDWIG VAN BEETHOVEN****, my ***IRISH SETTER**** ate most of our wheat and barley, and my mom studied ***ARCHIMEDES'**** mathematical concepts. She also read a great deal of poetic novels written by ***JOHN STEINBECK**** and studied ancient fossils that could possibly exist beneath our farm. Dad was sort of looney and tried some really stupid things, such as killing and skinning ***DIAMONDBACK RATTLESNAKES****. My brother, whom I consider mentally retarded, stayed inside his room practicing his stupid ***HINDU RELIGION OF YOGA****. And me, well, I would usually just lie in the fields of gold and waste time and listen to the mockingbirds mock the crows. Sometimes, though, it would seem that they were laughing at me because of the same white shirt and same hole-infested pants that I wore every day. **Researched Information*

The ***SUN SHONE***** upon the leather from our cow's hide as it rose above the ***BRISTLE-POINTED TREETOPS*****. The ***WIND FLAPPED THE LEATHER***** that held together my moccasins, and the ***BERMUDA GRASS OF REFRESHING GREEN SWAYED*****. The quail that lived by my pond ***SHATTERED MY EARDRUMS***** with the awful noise that only they made, and ***ICICLE CHIPS***** would constantly ***FLOW IN A STREAM RUNNING DOWN MY SPINE*****. ***Imagery*

"Mom, I'm going to meet Beethoven, I mean Benny, at the pond. I'll be home sometime tonight," I said.

"Okay, but be careful. Remember Jacob, after the first death there is no other."

I took my daily stroll down the path of darkness and knew that at the other end would be two friends waiting, Benny and ***THE POND***. As I looked ahead upon the ground, watching for potholes, I saw the ***ZINNIAS SWAYING IN THE WIND***** and ***HEARD THE UMBRELLA BIRD CRYING***** its awful cry, and the ***WIND COOLED MY FACE***** from the immense heat. ***Imagery*

At last I arrived, ***DISCOVERING AN UNIMAGINABLE SIGHT***. My head started spinning, my mouth started watering, the wind cooled my face from the immense heat as Benny introduced me to Renea. ***MY KNEES SUDDENLY FELT LIKE RUBBER*** as my hands got clammy, and the wind tried to cool my face from the immense heat.

After I finally pulled myself together, Benny introduced me to Renea.

This girl wasn't just one of those typical everyday, semi-pretty passersby that you see in school all the time. After debating over what we were going to do for the next thirty minutes, we decided to climb the holm oak tress at the beginning of the path towards Benny's house.

We started walking, but of course, Benny had to be the first one up, so he dashed toward it. Renea trailed behind, keeping her distance, but making sure she didn't fall too far behind. By the time I arrived at the foot of the tree, Benny was already half-way up, acting ***AS THOUGH HE WERE A GORILLA*** swinging from forest to forest. Renea followed behind him, but again keeping her distance. As I started climbing the tree, a branch that Renea was standing on gave away and she fell with it, ***CRYING A SCREAM OF DEATH LIKE SATAN CALLING A DEMON***. ***ACTING UPON INSTINCT***, I leaped forward onto the ground and broke her fall, but her head still hit hard on the green concrete, ***KNOCKING HER UNCONSCIOUS***.

This was the moment I had waited for all of my life; I was holding ***THE MOST BEAUTIFUL GIRL I HAD EVER SEEN IN MY ENTIRE LIFE***, not including my mother. There was one slight problem, though, that made me wish that this hadn't happened. What should I have done? Should I have put her down and let her gain consciousness or keep holding her until she woke up? This was a Kodak moment that I would remember, especially because of not knowing what to do. My mind fluttered off into a million directions, some thoughts good, some ordinary, and some unmentionable.

Benny, apparently in shock, quickly pulled her out of my arms and dragged her to the edge of the pond and smothered her face with water. He continued scooping the water in an unnecessary panic.

After splashing ***MILLIONS OF GALLONS*** of mud-stained pond water on her face, she gained consciousness. Benny was just about as relieved as Renea was to find that we had saved her.

I wish now, that Benny had never brought Renea to the pond. I had planned on swimming or something like that, W-I-T-H-O-U-T someone else tagging along. A perfect planned-out day was ruined by one stupid little girl.

HAVING DECIDED TO PADDLE OUT IN THE POND WITH OUR HOMEMADE CANOE, we started nearing the middle, the deepest area. I asked to head back, but they just made fun of me and started rocking the canoe. In a split second, it tipped over and ***"CRRAACKKK."***

That all happened, oh, about three days ago, and now I'm here in my room with nothing to do. I am forbidden to go back to the pond, and it'll be a few ***BED-LYING DAYS*** before I am allowed to see Benny again.

My mom explained to me that I had fallen out of the canoe and hit my head on a rock. Evidently the rock overcame my ability to survive

consciousness and I passed out when my oxygen passage was cut off by the water. Luckily Benny knows some lifesaving skills and dragged me out. Then he ran and got my dad.

Now I'm in bed with only a memory to work with. *THE SUN STILL SHINES UPON THE FIELDS OF GOLD, THE WIND STILL GRASPS THE IMMENSE HEAT** from the earth, cooling it down to a mere 100 degrees, *DAD STILL TENDS THE FARM**** and drives the livestock almost as crazy as he is, *MOM STILL MAKES, IN DAD'S WORDS, "THE MOST LUSCIOUS, MOUTH-WATERING PIE IN THIS HERE COUNTY,"**** *THE DOG STILL CHEWS**** on our half-eaten crops, *BENNY STILL WAITS**** at the pond thinking that I'l be healed in a day, like a miracle sent from God or something, and me, the only living person in the entire universe that can't still do his daily routine, lies here in bed with only memories to think about. Now, as my eyes slowly close, and my mind drifts into Never-Never Land, I fall into a deep, relaxing sleep of passing time.**

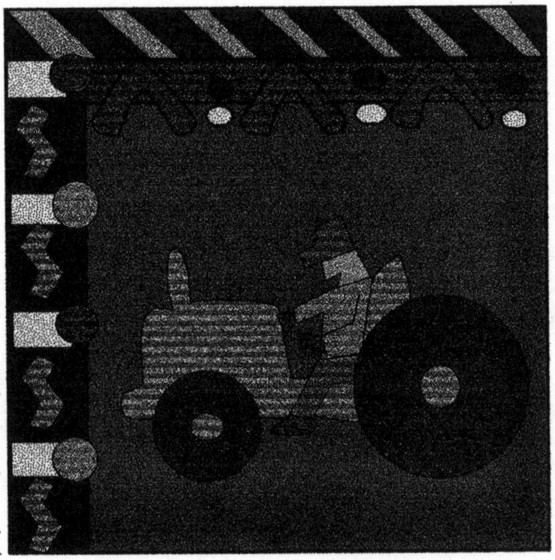

****Full-Circle Ending*

Jabari Phillips

Narrative Research Paper

Creature Teacher

I remember it well. Sitting there in that third-grade classroom and listening to other people get in trouble, I would always hear the teacher say, "You think it's funny now, but it won't be in fourth grade. You won't get a second chance."

I bet all of Highlands, Texas, could hear her. It was bad enough that the Persian Gulf War was going on, but this teacher made that seem like a little disagreement.

"You just wait and see; fourth grade will be one of the hardest grades in elementary. You won't be pampered day and night. You just wait and see!"

All throughout third grade, rumors about the best and worst teachers of the year were flying. One of the strictest, most cold-hearted, most mean-spirited, and most bad-tempered of all of Satan's children--Mrs. Eastbrook--was the topic of conversation. She made the Chinese earthquake that killed 830,000 (Bennett 11) look like a bad thought, or so they said. Anyway it went, I didn't want her as a teacher. Not at all.

The big day arrived. The first day of the rest of my life. The first day of fourth grade. As I stood there in line waiting to get my schedule card, I saw several children cry out loud when they saw their card. I almost forgot the two other "evil teachers" who taught there. Once I was handed my card, I took a sheet of notebook paper, folded it, and put it up to my schedule card. I was probably more tense than the 162,708 Americans that died in the Korean War (Gardner 384). I uncovered the first line. It read: C. Hicks. Now that my heart was beating again, I uncovered the second and third line: science and math--C. Hicks. I pulled the whole sheet off. It read: spelling, reading, language, and homeroom--A. Eastbrook.

I would have killed myself if I weren't already dead. I just stood there motionless, speechless, and lifeless. There was no telling what I would have done if two of my friends hadn't come to tell me that they had Mrs. Eastbrook too.

I walked down that hall, feeling like I had been shot with an elephant gun, or wishing I had. When I looked at my card, for a second time, the name "Eastbrook" seemed to have an eerie glow as it burned through the card.

I came to a branch in the hallway. It seemed happier in the rooms 120-130 branch. There was something sinister about the rooms 131-139. I looked at my card: Eastbrook--room 135. I really expected that.

As soon as I walked into the room, I noticed the smell before anything else. It was a musty attic, dirty socks, and outdoors combination with a hint of cheese. It made me wish I had one of those coin-operated oxygen machines like they had in Tokyo ("Tokyo" 3159). But I couldn't think about the smell now. Mrs. Eastbrook was standing in front of me, shaking the hands of the kids that had come in before me. I could just see her spreading some vile secretion through the pores on her huge, sweaty, twisted claws.

When it was my turn to "shake hands," I looked into her face, and I could have laughed. The last time I saw a face like that, I was watching The Predator. I held it in and took a seat, a seat as far away from her desk as possible.

Once everybody was seated, the announcements came on. It was the same old first-day-of-school talk: Welcome, Newcomers. Welcome back, Old-comers. Check with the office, Late-comers. I'm your principal. Blah, Blah, Blah, Blah.

As soon as announcements were over, Mrs. Eastbrook was at the head of the class going over rules, expectations, conduct, consequences, and assignment forms.

We had to write down her stupid classroom rules, all thirty-eight of them. She hovered over us like Hitler when he addressed a Nazis party in Harzburg in 1931 ("Hitler" 176). She told us that we would have homework everyday, which would include spelling words (ten times each), vocabulary (probably ten million of them), reading workbook pages (oh, fun), and D.O.L. (Deadly Overdose of Language).

After her grim introduction, she started right off with the teaching. She passed out the world-renowned language books, the ones that look like two cents but the ones we have to pay thirty dollars when we inevitably lose them. Then, she started reviewing the class on something about pronoun usage, something she said the whole class should have been taught by now, something that I--naturally--hadn't been.

Suddenly she spun her green, gnarled finger at me. "You!" she snarled, her eyes wide. "And your name is?"

"Jabari," I gasped, still in shock that she had picked me.

"You will read the first two paragraphs and answer the sample question. Aloud!"

The air became as still as death. The entire room seemed to stare down on me as I began to read.

"Stop there!" she screeched, as if I didn't know where to stop. "Now the sample question at the bottom of the page," Mrs. Eastbrook rasped slyly.

I looked at the sample question. Somebody had circled "B" as the answer. I had a real problem now. I could guess , or I could take that "B." I had to pull myself together, besides I knew the saying: "Fear is a noose that binds us until it strangles" (Toomer 252). I took the "B," hoping it was right and that I wouldn't look like a fool.

"Correct," Mrs. Eastbrook murmured, looking somewhat disappointed.

She gave us our language homework and then assigned our reading books. She gave us our reading homework and then she assigned our spelling books. Set, the Egyptian sun god of evil (Nault 113) didn't stand a chance against this evil woman, this inhuman thing, this, this...Creature Teacher.

My third grade teacher had been right, we wouldn't get a second chance, at least for now. I felt about as smart as that Pygmy chimp that could understand English (Linden 57). "This teacher feeds on carrion and small animals," I thought to myself. "She's a vulture" (Scott 182).

Right before I was about to go out of my mind, the bell rang. It was time to go to math, science, and history. Those classes were taught by one of the nicest teachers in the school. She didn't ask questions like: Who was the twenty-first President of the United States? Bing! Chester Alan Arthur ("World Leaders" 1665). She was calm and understanding.

Before I knew it, the day was over. I had survived, and maybe--just maybe--so will everybody else who faces the Creature Teacher.

How to Use The Response Sheet for Research Paper

Research Paper Presented to Whole Class

1. Ask students to make **two final drafts** of their research papers, one to be included in the teacher packet, the other to be read aloud by the student.

2. **Allowing class time**, interspersed with other class activities, for students to read their research papers in class has the following **advantages:**

   A. Student work can be used as **"literature,"** thus producing more "ownership" on the student's part and verifying for all students that student-written work has merit.

   B. The presentation can serve to **highlight literary terms, state-mandated test objectives, grammatical rules, etc.** to which the "audience" can respond on their "Response Sheet for Research Paper" (e.g. Section regarding literary terms and problem areas).

   C. Most districts require that students make a certain number of **oral presentations** per grading period/semester; hence, the research narrative could help satisfy this requirement.

   D. As the student reads, **the teacher can mark errors**, not only saving time for the teacher, but providing **immediate feedback** to the writer as well as reinforcing skills for the class as a whole. Outlining, bibliographies, etc. can be checked more thoroughly later.

Small Group Presentations

1. If your situation does not allow for whole group presentations, **small group response** may use the same format of the "Response Sheet for Research Paper." For instance, four students could read each other's papers silently, responding in writing.

2. Or students can read the papers in a **Musical Chair method**, each class member moving to another student's desk, responding to the paper at that desk.

Oral Grading of Response Sheets

1. The teacher may call on students, asking for various responses from the "Response Sheet for Research Paper."

2. Students respond on the sheet as the writer reads; then the teacher may ask one student (or several students) to **read** from their "Response Sheet for Research Paper" regarding **what they liked about the narrative**. Another student (or several students, each of whom might have slightly different answers) may be called on to give, for instance, a rising action, climax, falling action.

3. These may be **entered as class grades of 10 or 20 points** and serve not only to help students become **active listeners** but also to **reinforce various skills** for the class as a whole. Discussions can ensue regarding effective stylistic devices, literary terms, problem areas, etc.

Name of Responder:____________________ Name of Writer:________________

Class:______________________________ Date:________________________

Response Sheet for Research Paper

I. Narrative

A. Explain what you liked about the narrative itself.

____

____

B. List a **rising action, climax, and falling action** of the narrative:

1. **Rising Action:**________________________________
2. **Climax:**____________________________________
3. **Falling Action:**______________________________

II. Stylistic Devices

Stylistic Devices--List three of the **best sentences/passages**, ones that were particularly descriptive, well-written, etc.

A.____

B.____

C.____

III. Facts

Facts--List three **interesting researched facts** the author used:

A.____

B.____

C.____

IV. Literary Terms

Literary Terms--List examples of the **three literary terms** that the student author or your teacher targeted for this paper:

A. Term:_____________**Evidence**:______________________________

B. Term:_____________**Evidence**:______________________________

C. Term:_____________**Evidence**:______________________________

V. Problem areas--As your teacher chooses three **problem areas, correct** them on the lines below:

A.____

B.____

C.____

VI. Comments about presentation

A. Explain specifically what you **liked about the presentation itself.** (You could include any "extras" that the author used.)

____

____

B. What could the author have done to **improve his/her presentation**?

____

____

VII. Grade

A. What **grade** would you give the author?__________________________

B. Explain your **reasoning** by using examples:_______________________

____

How to Use Narrative Tests

1. The **"Library Book Test/ Narrative Vignette"** is designed to give students practice in *narrowing down important incidents in their novels, choosing one of these incidents, and retelling it from another character's perspective.*

   ➜ Students will not only be forced to think of the **impact of the incident** from a different angle but will be required to use the **language of the text** as well.

2. The **"Short Story Research Test"** is one method of testing students over narrative/research techniques. After students have completed their narrative research paper, the test can be used as a **unit final exam**, which requires that students understand various aspects of *writing narratives* as well as the *intricacies of research.*

Name:________________________ Class:______________ Date:______________

Library Book Test Narrative Vignette

Bibliographic Entry: ____

____

____

For Ray Bradbury's novel Dandelion Wine, a reader could remember many incidents, several of which might be the following:

1. John Huff moves;
2. Miss Fern and Miss Roberta think they have killed Mr. Quartermain in their Green Machine;
3. Douglas persuades Mr. Sanderson to let him work for the price of new tennis shoes.

For your book, brainstorm three incidents that you remember:

1.____

2.____

3.____

Your job is to choose one of the incidents in your book and retell it from a different person's point of view.

For instance, the John Huff incident is told in an omniscient point of view. You could choose to write from Doug's or John's viewpoint.

Rubric:

1. **Style--** **Obviously you will be retelling a section of the book; the incident will not be yours, but the language will. You will be graded on your style, your writing ability, your use of figurative language--in other words, the interest level.**

2. **Form--Write your vignette as if it is happening now, which means in the present tense. You will not be a student summarizing a section of a book; you will be giving a slice-of-life, a piece of a character's life as if it were happening right before our eyes.**

3. **Mechanics--Write freely, revise and edit. Watch for the following:**

   a. Run-ons

   b. Fragments

   c. Present tense--be consistent

   d. Spelling

YOU MAY NOT USE YOUR BOOK FOR ANY PART OF THIS TEST.

Name:________________________Class:_____________________Date:_______________

Short Story/ Research Test

1. List three ways an author might **begin a narrative**. Give a **short example** of each technique.

   A. Method #1:________________________

   B. Method #2:________________________

   C. Method #3:________________________

2. Most short stories (narratives) contain **dialogue**. Rewrite the following dialogue using the **correct punctuation, capitalization, and paragraph division.**

Fishing trip? I asked, surprised and delighted to go somewhere. Yeah he answered mine and Jason's. Oh I said in a flat, hopeless voice.

3. Writers of short stories need to be aware of their **verb tenses** so as not to confuse their readers. Rewrite the following paragraph so that all verbs will be in the **past tense. Circle the verbs that you change.**

We pulled up to Clear Lake Intermediate School, and the whole bus is astonished. The junior high is two stories and huge! We get off the bus and carry our instruments into the cafeteria, which is to be our warm-up room. It is like a sea of musical instruments, people, and noise. Lots of noise! We find our assigned table and sit down. I carefully pull my horn out of its case and warm up.

4. Sometimes writers need to do **research** to make their short stories more believable, more authentic. Rewrite the following excerpt from a student paragraph to include an **internal footnote** in the appropriate place. Pretend that the author's name is **A.R. Smith** and that the information came from **page 112.**

In Houston, one more time, I performed yet another routine. Houston's 300 parks and the Astrodome could not begin to hold my excitement.

5. Most short stories contain a **plot** that can be graphed on a **plot graph**. Draw a plot graph and place **eight significant events from your day yesterday**. You may not divide your events by first period class, second period, etc. Think of the eight most important things that happened, dividing them into six rising actions, one climax, and one falling action.

6. Most writers choose to make their writing more interesting by using **figurative language** (e.g., similes, metaphors, personification, etc.). Identify the type of figurative language in the following student passages

_______________ a. We were on the runway, taking off from zero miles per hour to what seemed like billions.

_______________ b. The palm trees were coming off their winter diets and becoming rather large.

_______________ c. I kept running, and when I reached the log in the middle of the road, I leaped it like Lewis's record-breaking long jump.

_______________ d. To me, the so-called "Golden State" is an overpopulated wasp's nest.

_______________ e. The world stops then and there. Every eye, every ear, every civilized being on Earth turns a head in the direction of 11th Street.

7. Writers need to know about **research techniques**. Answer the following questions in **short sentences**.

   A. What is **plagiarism**?______________________________________

   B. What is a **Bibliography or a Works Cited**?______________________________________

   C. How do **internal footnotes** differ from **end notes**?______________________________________

   D. What is the purpose of **footnotes**?______________________________________

   E. Why does a writer need to make a **rough draft**?______________________________________

8. Give **three specific areas** for which you as a writer might need to **proofread/revise** your paper. Give a **brief example** of each. (Note: anything already mentioned on this test may not be used.)

   A. Area #1:________________ Example:____________________________

   B. Area #2:________________ Example:____________________________

   C. Area #3:________________ Example:____________________________

Answers to:

Short Story/ Research Test

1.

A. Dialogue: "You watch your step, boy...you messin' with the wrong one...you better think again, boy...you fightin' fire."

Virgil flung out the words like a kid throwing tinsel on a Christmas tree--all in one bright silver ball. Not a careful placement, shiny strand by shiny strand, sentence by sentence. It seemed a cross between wanting to be interested, wanting to do it up right, but being a little bored by it.

B. Description: He's wearing a sweater, caramel-colored I think. And reclining against something. Deep cushions. Down maybe. His shoes are off and his cashmere socks look soft, sensual. And the thing is I can't see me, except my bare feet and bent knees. I think I must be in some chair or on the floor, I don't really remember. See, I can't see me. Just him.

C. Conflict: Like all Southern mothers, my mother had determined early in our relationship that no matter what it took-- all the family money, all the family patience, or with my stiff, white petticoats raised, all the swift lashes Mother could bring herself to administer with the family switch--I would learn one thing or they, and presumably I, would die trying. I would learn how to be a lady. A Southern lady.

★ Answers will vary as to methods that can be used.

2.

"Fishing trip?" I asked, surprised and delighted to go somewhere.

"Yeah," he answered, "mine and Jason's."

"Oh," I said in a flat, hopeless voice.

3. was, was, got, carried, was, was, found, sat, pulled, warmed

4. Houston's 300 parks and the Astrodome (Smith 112) could not begin to hold my excitement.

5. Answers will vary according to student.

6.

A. Hyperbole
B. Personification
C. Simile
D. Metaphor
E. Hyperbole

7.

A. Plagiarism is copying more than three or four words in succession from a text without giving attribution.

B. A Bibliography or Works Cited is a list of sources used in a research paper.

C. Internal footnotes are within the text and include only the author's last name and the page number of the information; end notes are at the bottom of the text and include bibliographic information.

D. The purpose of footnotes is to give credit to the source from which the quoted or paraphrased information came.

E. A writer needs to make a rough draft to get his/her ideas down before attempting revision, proofreading, etc.

8. Answers will vary.

PART III

PERSUASIVE RESEARCH

Using Independent Reading Persuasive Support

1. **The Independent Reading Persuasive Support** assignment prepares students to think persuasively by asking them to *cite three specific reasons* that their library/independent reading book (or their class-assigned novel) is one they would *recommend or not recommend.*

2. Students must then choose **quotations from the text that support their reasoning**, thus persuading the reader that their *thesis*--recommending the book or not recommending it--is a sound one.

3. In **preparation for a paper that includes quoted support**, ask students to *explain their choices*, which later--in a paper--would be *blended with the quoted material itself.*

Name:______________________ Class:______________ Date:________________

Independent Reading Persuasive Support

Bibliographic Entry for Library Book:________________________________

____.

Assignment:

1. As you read, think of **three specific reasons** why you like (or don't like) your book.

2. As support for each reason, **quote three passages** from your book that **prove** your reasoning. Be sure to include an internal footnote and remember the rules for quoting dialogue.

3. In your own words, **explain each passage** in terms of **why the quoted material acts as support for your reasoning.**

I. Reason #1:__________________________

A. Support

1. Quote:____

____

2. Explanation:____

____

____

B. Support

1. Quote: ______________________________

____

2. Explanation: ______________________________

____

____

C. Support

1. Quote: ______________________________

____

2. Explanation: ______________________________

____

____

II. Reason #2: ______________________________

A. Support

1. Quote: ______________________________

____

2. Explanation: ______________________________

____

____

B. Support

1. Quote: ______________________________

____

2. Explanation: ______________________________

____

____

C. Support

1. Quote: ______________________________

____

2. Explanation: ______________________________

____

____

III. Reason #3: ______________

A. Support

1. Quote: ______________________________

____

2. Explanation: ______________________________

____

____

Independent Reading: Persuasive Support

B. Support

1. Quote:____

____

2. Explanation:____

____

____

C. Support

1. Quote:____

____

2. Explanation:____

____

____

Using "You Are the Author"

1. After students have finished reading their **individual library books**, assign an **in-class essay test** over the book.

2. "You Are the Author" works well in conjunction with a **persuasive writing unit** or as a review of that mode and gives students a chance not only to role play but to present their evidence/support in a more creative format.

3. Skills such as **summarization** and **tense consistency**, among others, are a focus.

Name:____________________ Class:__________ Date:________________

You Are the Author!

Problem Solving:

You are the author of your book and are scheduled on a book tour in several major cities to promote your latest work. Your first scheduled stop is in Houston at the Brazos Bookstore. The setting for the evening, you're told, will be a formal reading for approximately 100 people. You will be expected to speak for one hour, reading from three of the best sections of your book. Prior to your arrival, though, the bookstores want a summary of each section from which you will take your excerpts.

Assignment:

Write a proposal in the format of a five-paragraph essay explaining which sections you will choose and why. Your purpose is to convince bookstore owners that you have an interesting evening planned in that the sections you have chosen are certain to capture the attention of the audience. Be creative! Be convincing! Be specific!

Do your brainstorming/webbing on the back of this sheet, which you will attach to your rough draft and final papers.

- ✏ Remember to use present tense when writing about literature.
- ✏ Proofread for fragments, run-ons, spelling, etc.

Allisa Brill
You Are the Author
Library Book Test
Persuasive Mode

The Ordinary Princess

Dearest Mr. Fred Banda,

If you are wondering why so formal, I still haven't forgiven you. That was my piece of writing and you knew it! Sure, you say, but that was a long time ago. Maybe for you, but fourth grade wasn't that long ago for me...But like you say, that is in the past now. Somehow I will find it in my heart to forgive you. Until then, you owe me one. A while back you mentioned that you were working at the Brazos Bookstore and that many famous authors come to give book reviews. Well, I might find room in my heart if you could get me to talk about my new book there in Houston. I titled this creation of mine **The Ordinary Princess**. I keep reading it over and over, and each time I read it I get a new favorite part. So far I've got three, all of which are entertaining, humorous, and romantic. Let me tell you about my story.

First, I'll describe the very best part, how **entertaining** it is. The main character is a princess named Amethyst, but because of a gift from a fairy, she is very ordinary-looking. For this reason, everyone just calls her Amy. All of her sisters have recently been married, and her parents are trying their hardest to find poor Amy a husband. When worst comes to worst, the King decides to **hire a dragon** and stow his precious daughter away in a tower. The **brave knight** who defeats the cold-hearted beast will win Princess Amethyst's hand in marriage. Amy catches wind of this and doesn't agree with it one bit! She decides to leave the castle and run away to the forest, where she has already made secret excursions. In the **Forest of Faraway**, the Princess befriends a young red squirrel and a black-as-night crow. Amy thoroughly enjoys her new home in the forest. But, happiness is not everlasting. Soon, Amethyst's dress grows ragged and is literally hanging by threads. After trying everything she can to fix it up, she becomes very downcast. Then, the fairy that gave her her ordinary looks comes to the rescue by telling Amy to go to the nearby town and **get work** there so she can earn enough money to buy a new dress. So, off she goes, with her squirrel and crow in tow. Soon, a castle comes into view. But can you imagine--Princess Amethyst, a kitchen maid? I told you this book of mine is entertaining.

Next, **The Ordinary Princess** has **humorous parts** in it as well. While Amy works at the castle, a princess comes to visit the young king there. He, too, is looking for a key to fit his lock. On the day this princess arrives, a banquet is held in her honor. Amethyst is kept busy in preparation for days. After the celebration, Amy sneaks into the empty ballroom to steal a few nuts for her animal companions. Only then does she notice the dark figure on one of the center tables. She confronts this man and asks of his occupation. It is obvious to him she is a **kitchen maid,** and he tells her he is a **man-of-all-work,** though we know this isn't true. Who else could it be other than the King himself? How humorous to think of the two sitting and eating melting ice cream and confiding in each other everything but what is most important.

Last, let me tell you why I think the story is so **romantic.** Eventually, the prince and princess figure out each other's true status, and everything just clicks into place. He gives her a quick **proposal**, and Amy quickly answers with an exuberant "Yes!" Amy travels back to her home castle, and hugs are generously passed around at her return. She anxiously waits until a few months later when her husband-to-be asks her father for her hand. Of course, Amy can't let on that she met the King before, and she does a good job in pretending. Then, the next April, they are **married.** For their **honeymoon** they should go away to one of the rooms in the King's castle, but instead, they travel to their **forest.** Do you like the ending, Fred?

So everything will end up hunky-dory between us, Fred, if you let me talk about my entertaining, humorous, and romantic story at the Brazos Bookstore.

Name:________________________Class:_________________Date:_________________

Persuasive Library Book Test

Assignment:

1. You have just read about a **contest for a teen magazine** that asks you to **persuade readers** to read a particularly good book. The catch is that you must persuade them in **poem form**!

2. When you read the fine print, you discover even more: your word count must be between **100 and 200 words**, the review itself must be placed on an **index card** (front and back) and it must be **illustrated**.

Problem Solving:

1. You must try to persuade readers to want to read your book; therefore, you must **consider your audience** and what might interest them.

2. You also must convince the judges that you have read your book, which means that you must **include at least ten specific details from the book**, however not those that will give away crucial points of plot that might spoil the book's climax.

3. You must **proofread** your work, especially for the following:
   - a. Present tense (Remember to write about literature in the present tense.)
   - b. Poem form (free verse--not rhymed)
   - c. Spelling

4. Be sure to include the **author, title, and type of fiction** (e.g., adventure, romance, science fiction, horror, realism, historical, humorous, etc.).

Restrictions:

1. You **may refer to your book** but **not to any tests/notes/etc.**
2. You will have only **one period** to complete the written portion of the assignment.
3. Some sort of **illustration** must be used.

Teacher Example:

Bradbury, Ray. Dandelion Wine.

Douglas, the pretend magician
boy-turning-man
afraid of his own mortality

Hadn't John Huff, best of all friends,
left
vanished in the night
John
"the only god living"
in Green Town, Illinois,
summer of 1928
John who could pathfind
and cowboy-sing
and swing from vine to vine

And hadn't Great-Grandmother died
no more roof-sitting
or rug-cleaning
or park-running
But then no one really dies having had
a family she had said
as the final wave washed her to shore

But hadn't the Time Machine
told his last story
Ching Ling Soo and
Pawnee Bill and
"the grand armies of ancient prairies"
lost, never again to rumble in little boys' minds

Persuasive Library Book Test

And the Lonely One
hadn't he ruined the ravine
that fine and lovely playhouse
for boys wishing to be Indians
or Indians wishing to be boys
who stay out too late
while Mamas iron
and little brothers sit at screened doors
and watch

But the other Douglas, the real magician,
boy-turned-man
no longer afraid

Restored Grandma's kitchen
Saved her from Aunt Rose
Topsy-turvied spices and flours and relishes
Reinvented Thursday night specials
Made of ingredients eyes
cannot see

This Douglas
Freed Miss Fern and Rose from their attic prison
Yelling street-side that their worst fear in reality
Only fiction
No man had died from their Green Machine
after all

And what about the Tarot Witch
a carnival's wax dummy,
Doug's special lady,
used to spitting out fortunes for lonely souls
for those who believed
a target now for Mr. Black's wrath
pulled from the fate of the ravine
alive once more

Douglas
an entrepreneur in tennis shoes that jump
rivers and trees and houses

a romantic preserving the silence
fit for the love of the century
a boy who will drink in the April air
the autumn breezes and Antilles wind
a survivor who will record it all
yellow Ticonderoga pencil in hand
the magician's wand still waving
no longer "crushed down by the great weight of summer"

Kelly Ochoa
Student Sample

Randle, Kristen. The Only Alien on the Planet. New York: Scholastic, 1995.

Because my name is Ginny Christianson
I guess it is written,
in some black, silent space,
that I will be moved to the East
before my senior year
NOW I'm not my jumping-for-joy,
heel-clicking
usual self
But at least I know I'm not
"the only alien on the planet"
Or so Paul assures me

Because Paul leaves,
my big brother,
protector of the galaxy,
no longer will we stay up all night
watching horror movies,
drowning in bucket loads
of white, fluffy popcorn
Now I must "take hold,"
"Attack" this new life
"the way you would a wild windmill"!

Because we move,
I meet Caulder,
a happy boy "with a wide mouth
used to smiling"
We share a special bond,
one only Hally can break

Because I meet Hally
my world becomes parties, people and places.
"Hally is a little Hellion"

yet only she can help me meet
Pete Zabriski by letting my
love-proclaiming note
be taken up by "Mrs. Eagle Eye"

Because I meet Smitty,
my life changes
The "most beautiful human being" with
His solitude, his silence amazing me
And as time goes on
Caulder and I crack into his emotions
Finding a "human" human being
someone real, not a joke
and he is awakening

"Smitty Tibbs has just graduated
from Interesting Problem to
full frighteningly Human Being"
because my name is Ginny
because Paul leaves
because we move
because I meet Caulder and Hally
And Smitty, who's
most definitely not
the only alien on the planet

Rachel Brown
Student Sample

Cooney, Caroline B. Out of Time. New York: Bantam, 1996.

Annie Lockwood, a lovesick puppy,
misses her first true love
But one problem
her lover, her so-called maniac
is from another time,
a time where expensive furs
are in style,
furs that warm the soul

better than steaming bowls
of Campbell's soup

A place where money is a virtue
touching everything except true love,
a place where women wear bustles
and veils with divine sequined long dresses
just to show off,
a place where love is so compassionate
you have to be
an outcast and break down barriers
with your flirtatious looks
to save your century-crossed love

An adventure where you're Indiana Jones
pretending to be the doctor in charge,
putting on his clothes, his shoes,
being a spy, an outlaw
to save what you can't live without

A dream where your carriage
is waiting in the dreary snow,
colder than a black heart,
where you're on the run for your life
when suddenly with a jerk
the carriage stops
pulling a thousand deaths from you
where the police have cornered your heart
till it beats faster and faster still
as if it's running its last race
before it's Out of Time

How to Write an Argumentative/ Persuasive Research Paper

1. Prepare students for writing their **argumentative/persuasive research paper** by asking them to **brainstorm** a list of possible topics in which they are interested. The class as a whole could suggest **controversial categories** such as political, environmental, economic, social and moral issues to stimulate actual topic ideas.

2. Ask students to temporarily **choose one topic**, but to help ensure that students are not just choosing a topic randomly, ask them to do the following:
   A. List reasons why they are personally interested in the topic
   B. List facts they already know about the topic
   C. List specific questions they would like to learn about their topic

3. Then ask students to **discuss the issue with a partner**, formulating a **"working thesis and web."**

4. Students can make **Note Card Stations** at their desks by doing the following:
   A. Writing their working thesis statement on a card
   B. Writing each of three aspects on an individual card
   C. Listing any working subpoints on separate cards
   D. Displaying the cards in pyramid fashion, the thesis card at the top, all three aspects below it on the same "line," and any subpoints emanating from their aspects

5. Students can then move to each other's desks for the purpose of **commenting on the preliminary ideas expressed** and making any **suggestions** in terms of a line of argument, subpoints, flaws in reasoning, etc.

6. Finally ask students to find as much **information** as possible to bring to class to start the **research process** of reading, taking notes, abandoning some sources, adding others, etc. Or they should make a **list of possible sources** for their visit to the library.

Name:_____________________________**Class:**____________________**Date:**____________________

Syllabus for Argumentative/Persuasive Research Paper

Day One--Orientation

1. Take a sample note card for **books**, **encyclopedias**, **magazines**, and **CDROM/Internet.**

2. From your list of **brain stormed topics**, choose an issue you would like to **argue for or against. Remember** that research is like a **treasure hunt**; therefore, list only those topics that truly interest you, that you consider "treasures" to be discovered.

3. Make a **web** with the following:

   a. Put the **issue and the position** you are taking in the **central circle** (e.g., The federal government should provide more programs for the homeless).

   b. Brainstorm for your three main spokes three **possible reasons/points** that you could use in your argument.

   ➜ A trick is to ask yourself "Why?" If your thinking is logical, your answer will be "because..."

   c. Turn to your neighbor and **share your reasoning.** He/she might be able to lend some **insight** into the **direction** the argument could take before your initial research.

4. Begin initial research on your **first reason.**

Days Two and Three--Research First Reason

1. Begin taking **ten note cards on your first reason.**
   (E.g, The problem of homelessness is increasing.)

   a. Statistics on yearly increase in numbers
   b. Information about increase of types of homeless people
      1. Teenagers/runaways
      2. Battered women
      3. Elderly

2. If you come across any information that would fit into another one of your webbed reasons while you are working on this reason, **take the note and code it with the slug of the appropriate reason.**

3. At the beginning of day four, a **note card check** will be made to determine the **form and number** of your note cards.

Days Four and Five--Research Second Reason

1. Begin taking **ten note cards on your second reason.**
   (E.G., THE HOMELESS ARE INCREASINGLY BECOMING A PART OF SOCIETY'S PROBLEM:)
   A. CRIME
   b. Drugs
   c. ECONOMY

2. Again, if you find information that will fit in with any of your other reasons, **add the appropriate note card at that time.**

3. At the beginning of day six, a **note card check** will be made to determine the **form and number** of your note cards for this reason.

Days Six and Seven--Research Third Reason

1. Begin taking **ten note cards on your third reason.**
   (e.g., Providing for those less fortunate is the humane thing to do.)
   a. Documentation from Biblical sources
   b. Documentation of aid to other countries
   c. Documentation of other social programs

Days Eight and Nine--Catch-up days

1. Do a "**Write to Learn**" on where you stand with your research.
   A. Without looking at your notes, **free write** about your topic and the **specific support** you have researched so far. This should be like thinking out loud and should not involve any referring to your note cards.
   B. The purpose of this is for you to learn the **strengths and weaknesses** of your reasoning while you are still in the library and still in a position to **augment your findings.**
2. **Catch up** on any area you need more information about.
3. If you are caught up, you may take **more note cards** on any of your reasons for **extra credit.**

Day Ten--Synthesis

1. Do a **detailed web** of your reasons and support for the purpose of a **final check** for strengths, weaknesses, and direction of argument.
2. Do any **final research** you deem necessary.
3. **Thirty note cards** will be due at beginning of the week when we return to the classroom.

Teresa Phillips
Persuasive/Argumentative Research Paper

The Alternative Lives of Dogs: How They Can Benefit Mankind

Narrative Scenario Introduction

Down the street on the corner lives Gandolf with the elderly widow, Mrs. Phillips. He is her constant, breathing shadow. Both Gandolf and Mrs. Phillips are quiet, reserved neighbors, never bothering anyone. Age has taken its toll on Mrs. Phillips; she can't see or hear very well and at times even falls victim to seizures. Gandolf doesn't seem to notice, though. "Gan," as Mrs. Phillips calls him, helps her in whatever ways he can. He wakes her when her alarm goes off, alerts her to phone calls, and lets her know when someone is at the door. He even works with Mrs. Phillips's daughter as a therapist for area nursing homes and helps Mrs. Phillips's son as a volunteer for the fire department rescue team. His eyes full of adoration, he sometimes just sits and gazes at Mrs. Phillips. Everyone in the neighborhood knows Gandolf loves Mrs.Phillips very much. He is her guardian angel. He is her beloved golden retriever.

Gandolf--and other dogs like him--might sound unbelievable, too good to be true. Most of us probably would not think a mere dog capable of performing such important tasks; however, dogs should not be considered just playmates for children or hunting mates for men who work their calendars around when the "seasons" open and close.

[We need to train more dogs to move beyond neighborhood backyards and hunting trips, to play more active roles in their relationships with humans as guardians, therapists, and lifesavers.]

First Aspect

Dogs, like Gandolf, should increasingly be called on to serve as **guardians** to many children and adults, like Mrs. Phillips. Dogs can form an undeniable bond with their masters, and through this bond can be trained to protect their masters' lives. Dogs can also be taught to watch over their child masters as if they themselves are the parents, and when their masters are in need, the dog's guardianship role can emerge in remarkable ways. The disabled can even experience a form of care-giving from their service dogs as well.

Certainly we all know the adage of not trusting anyone who does not like children and dogs. The combination of children and pets is as accepted as peanut butter and jelly, apple pie and ice cream, virtually anything we hold near and dear to our hearts. However, many of us fail to realize that dogs can be taught to feel much more than just companionship toward a child. Dogs can be conditioned to feel as if they are a child's guardian, his protector. This bond dogs form with their child masters is not an unknown fact. Many films, such as Old Yeller, depict dogs attacking other animals and defending their child masters against harm. Roger A. Caras best describes the dogs' awareness of their masters when he states, "Our dogs are tuned to us like radar dishes, and we, like interstellar space, are constantly being probed" (227). We need only to examine the German shepherd who took on this role of guardian for the new baby of a family. Documented twice within a nine-month period, a dog, so attuned to the baby's soft, rhythmic breathing, frantically alerted the parents when the baby suddenly stopped breathing, twice saving the baby's life (Stieger 50-51).

Besides being a savior for children, dogs can feel an overwhelming need to guard disabled masters against danger. Since dogs can accurately predict the onset of an epileptic seizure, some people, like Mrs. Phillips, who are prone to these seizures, have dogs (Stieger 58). This was the case with one young girl when her German shepherd grabbed her hand and lead her to the couch until the seizure could pass. Furthermore, after the girl lay down, the dog actually jumped on top of her, with its ear close to the girl's face, to monitor her breathing throughout the duration of the seizure (Caras 103-108). This incident depicts how the dog is capable of closely watching its master, guarding him with the keenest of ears for the slightest detection of possible harm and then doing what it feels necessary to protect its master from danger. The blind as well can count on their extensively trained Seeing Eye dogs to alert help if their masters trip or fall and can't get up (Schwartz 67). The Seeing Eye dogs watch traffic, looking for a safe spot for their masters to cross (Boorer 116). The deaf, also, can depend on their Hearing Ear dogs to alert them to strange sounds of danger, like that of the smoke detector (Schwartz 79). All of these jobs service dogs are able to perform if they are trained properly.

Second Aspect

Other dogs play roles of therapists in nursing homes, hospice homes for the seriously or terminally ill, as well as in homes for the mentally ill. In human-care facilities like these, dogs--like Gandolf--offer special therapeutic treatment no human can match. Dogs have a way of encouraging life through their actions, thus promoting self-healing. Dogs also possess the uncanny ability to provide the unconditional love, acceptance, and sense of companionship for which people in care facilities seem to long.

For people in nursing homes, dogs are a source of therapy and comfort (Lagoni 347). There is an overwhelming loneliness people feel that comes from being secluded in nursing homes since many nursing home residents have been removed from their community and isolated from friends they've known most of their adult lives

(Schwartz 30). Being able to socialize with dogs brings back memories of when these elderly people were young, when life was good, and perhaps when they themselves had a dog. In one incident an elderly man broke months of total silence when he was introduced to a puppy. With tears in his eyes, he softly said, "`I had a puppy like this when I was a boy'" (Caras 201). Dogs can indeed make us feel "important" and "needed" (Caras 114), a feeling almost forgotten by many residents of nursing homes. Furthermore, when asked about nursing home, pet-facilitated therapy, Dr. Samuel A. Corson of the Ohio State University Department of Psychiatry stated,

> Use of the pets is not a cure but rather a facilitator. It doesn't cure old age, but we think it can bring these patients out emotionally so they think better of themselves and interact more effectively with others. And, it can bring them out physically because they often begin to romp or walk with the dogs. (Galton 21)

Encouraging life in residents who feel their lives are already over and pointless, dogs make a welcomed addition to the conventional methods of therapy used in alternative home-care institutions today.

Besides providing a service for nursing home residents, dogs--like Gandolf--can serve as excellent therapists in many hospice homes for the seriously or terminally ill. Visits from the dogs provide something the patients can look forward to, offering entertainment and welcomed distractions from the patient's pain and infirmity (Blakeman 1). Many cancer wards already rely on dogs as a source of therapy for their patients; the dogs bring back the life and humor to the patient's dull and drab sense of existence (Steiger 60). Likewise, people with AIDS are also taking advantage of the therapeutic aspects of the dog's unconditional love and acceptance. One AIDS patient stated it plainly and simply, " 'When people are afraid to touch you, it is no small thing that your dog is there to nuzzle your hand and be petted' " (PAWS 1). The same is true for many people with serious or terminal illnesses. Most people don't want any physical contact with seriously or terminally ill patients, out of fear that they too will acquire the dreaded illness. Dogs, however, don't seem to pay attention to someone's illnesses or physical ability; instead they tend to accept people as they are (Caras 54). The dogs bring friendship and laughter to other people (PAWS 1), making the addition of dogs to conventional therapy a wonderful source of encouragement to the patients.

Not only can dogs be trained to help in nursing homes and hospices, they can also make effective therapists for the mentally ill who have withdrawn from the world around them. Dogs can serve as ice-breakers, inviting the ill back into reality. The Ohio State University Psychiatric Hospital reports that a 19-year-old psychotic boy, withdrawn and completely unresponsive to drugs or conventional therapy, was brought a small, wirehair fox terrier. Soon the boy began talking to the dog, doctors, and other patients, as well as moving about with the dog and participating in social activities. The boy opened up to therapy, recovered, and eventually was discharged all because of the introduction of the terrier to his therapy (Galton 21). Prisons, as well, are taking advantage of the use of dogs as therapy. Prison authorities say that the reclusive criminally insane respond to the dogs. The prisoners usually "assume full care" of the dogs and slowly "regain awareness of their own environments" (Schwartz 91). Dogs are able to bring out remarkable changes in the mental state of people and are a tool of therapy for the mentally ill.

Despite the views of some facilities that have policies against dogs, referring to them as unclean, unsafe or merely inappropriate (Blackman 2), the positive results of dog-related therapy should cause them to take a closer look at their policies and possibly make a change. In these human-care facilities, **the dogs bring patients a new sense of self-esteem and a will to get better**, as well as the ability to help them to see that life is precious and sacred. The dogs, if given the chance, could drastically improve therapy results of patients in nursing homes, hospice homes, and facilities for the mentally ill. Better therapy results in care facilities like these could mean that people will have shorter stays in the facilities and that people will live happier lives.

Third Aspect

Besides dogs as guardians and therapists, dogs can play roles of lifesavers for their human companions. Dogs not only save the lives of their masters, but there are **many dogs that work regularly with rescue teams**, sometimes saving several human lives at one time. Dogs in many K-9 units also work in conjunction with police and other law enforcement agencies to preserve the lives of humans. During these lifesaving events and tasks, dogs utilize their many magnified senses of smell, hearing, and raw intuition of danger to benefit their human companions.

Dogs are **faithful to their masters**, much like the way Gandolf is faithful to Mrs. Phillips. Dogs even feel sympathy for their master's pain (Steiger 48). One dog exemplified this faithfulness when, upon her master having a paralyzing stroke, she brought him water at his call for help by filling her mouth with water from her water bowl and then releasing snoutfuls of water into his mouth, keeping her master alive for nine days until he was found (Steiger 47-49). In another incident, a Maltese-poodle mix, sensing his master was in danger, went to inconceivable lengths to save his master's life. While taking a bath, his master had an asthma attack, blacked out, and slipped beneath the soapy water in the bathtub. The dog, in an effort to save his master, jumped into the bathtub, dove his head under the water like a duck, and pulled the tub stopper, releasing the water to drain. When the dog's master woke up, she was coughing up soapy water in a drained tub, the dog jumping up and down on her chest with the stopper in his mouth as if to say, "Wake up, I saved you! Wake up; I saved you!" (Steiger 179). These many lifesaving feats also include dogs waking their human families in the middle of the night to lead them to safety when their houses caught fire and filled with black smoke (Steiger 171-178). These examples of heroism prove that when the dogs could have just lain there and watched their masters die, they, instead, chose to perform lifesaving feats to keep their masters alive--because the dogs chose to do so.

In addition to a dog's saving its master's life, **many extensively trained dogs work with rescue teams**--like Roger's--searching for lost children and adults and finding disaster victims buried in the debris of an explosion or earthquake (Schwartz 106-114). One dog, a 65-pound pit bull terrier, received the Ken-L Ration's Dog Hero of the Year Award when she got credit for "saving the lives of 30 humans, 29 dogs, 13 horses, and one cat" during the disastrous floods in Southern California in 1993 (Steiger 181). On another occasion, a rescue dog's keen sense of smell found a retarded man alive, completely covered in snow, after only minutes of searching when other rescuers spent hours hunting for the lost man (Schwartz 95-97).

In the same manner, **police and other law enforcement agencies take advantage of dogs' acute senses of sound, smell, and sight to protect the public from illegal drugs and potentially dangerous bombs** (Schwartz 112, 131). Most of the time, the general public is not aware of how K-9 dogs preserve their lives. Many air travelers don't realize that the planes they ride in are first thoroughly inspected by K-9 dogs for the presence of explosives (Schwartz 11). K-9 dogs also make their police more effective by adding keener hearing and the extraordinary powers of scent that the darkness does not affect, as well as instilling additional fear in the criminals, making it less likely the officers will get hurt or killed (Boorer 106). The K-9 dogs, so dedicated in their jobs, will even give up their lives for those of the officers (Schwartz 111). Knowing the many ways the K-9 dogs can help preserve and protect our lives should be evidence that even more dogs should be properly trained.

Narrative Scenario Conclusion

Gandolf, the wonder, dog, seems quite real now. Although it is unlikely that in reality one dog will play the role of guardian, therapist, and lifesaver in the extraordinary way Gandolf does, it is likely that several dogs, each specially trained, can be found doing work in nearby communities everywhere.

Dogs touch our lives in so many ways every day, comforting us, guarding us, and sometimes even saving our lives. We have hatefully referred to dogs as mutts, destroyed them every day in pounds across the country, and purposely dumped them off on the sides of our roads and highways. **[If we would realize that dogs can be specially trained as guardians, therapists, and lifesavers, mankind would surely benefit.]**

How to Use the Partner Check

1. After students have completed the rough draft of their research paper, ask them to choose a partner for the purpose of revision/proofreading. Students exchange drafts and answer the questions in the **Partner Rubric Check**. The authors of the papers may wish to have errors, suggestions, questions, etc. written on their drafts as well.

2. The **Partner Rubric Check** can be completed in stages. For instance, after the class has written their introductions, students may use a partner to assess only that aspect of the paper. Then, as each body of the paper is completed, partners can evaluate that section.

3. Students may complete the **Partner Rubric Check** on their own paper first then choose a partner to compare assessments.

Name:______________________________ Class:__________________ Date:____________________

Partner Rubric Check for Persuasive Research Paper

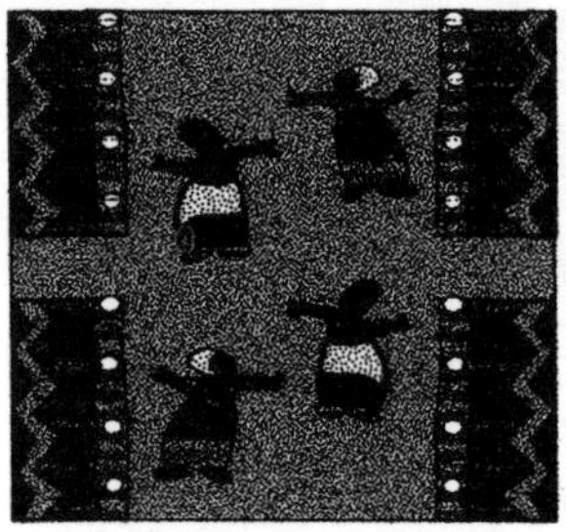

Author of Paper: ____

I. Introduction

A. State the thesis of the paper and the plan of development:

____

____

1. Are the verbs active?____________________

✏ List three active verbs:

A.____________________________

B.____________________________

C.____________________________

2. Are the **three points** to be covered stated in **parallel terms?**

____

✏ If so, label the parts, proving that they are indeed parallel. If not, correct the error by rewriting the sentence on this sheet.

A.____________________ (____________________)

B.____________________ (____________________)

C.____________________ (____________________)

B. How has the author used the **narrative/descriptive scenario** to **make the thesis more persuasive?**

____

____

C. List the **most effective sentence** in the scenario and explain its effect:

1. Sentence:________________________________

____

2. Effect:__________________________________

____

D. List the **least effective sentence/part of the scenario** and **explain** how it could be corrected. *(e.g., Maybe one part rambles or gets off the subject. Or maybe a part needs to be expanded* in order to "set the stage" for the author's reasoning that is to follow.)

1. **Sentence:** ______________________________

____

2. **Correction:** ______________________________

____

E. **List at least two sentences with grammatical problems and correct them.**

1. **Grammar problem #1**
   - **A. Sentence:** ______________________________
   - **B. Correction:** ______________________________

2. **Grammar problem #2**
   - **A. Sentence:** ______________________________
   - **B. Correction:** ______________________________

F. **If you were to grade the scenario alone, what letter grade would you give it and why?**

____

____

II. Body Paragraph

A. **In your own words, not the author's, state the idea the author is trying to convey in this section:**

____

____

B. **In your own words, list the most persuasive detail the author has used and explain how it supports the author's contention.**

1. Detail: ____

____

2. Explanation: ____

____

C. **In your own words, list the least effective detail and explain why it is not as persuasive as the rest.**

1. Detail: ____

____

2. Explanation: ____

____

D. **List any figurative language/description that adds interest to this section:**

1. ____

2. ______________________________

E. If the author needs **added interest**, list a part that could be reworded and reword it for him/her.

1. Problem: ______________________________

2. Revision: ______________________________

F. List two sentences with **grammatical problems** and correct them below:

1. Problem #1:

A. Sentence: ______________________________

B. Correction: ______________________________

2. Problem #2:

A. Sentence: ______________________________

B. Correction: ______________________________

G. What **grade** would you give this point and why?

____

____

III. Conclusion

A. How has the author used the concluding scenario to **benefit** the paper?

____

____

B. Did the author **restate the thesis** and the three main points?

____

C. List the most **effective sentence** in the conclusion.

____

____

D. **List the least effective** sentence and tell why.

____

____

E. List one sentence with a **grammatical problem** and correct it.

____

____

F. What **grade** would you give the conclusion and why?

____

____

Using Partner Check/ Research Rubric #2

1. **Partner Check /Research Rubric #2** is geared to assessing *sections of the research paper in stages*, not the research paper as a whole.

2. One effective method is to play **"Musical Chairs,"** asking students to leave that section of their research paper *(e.g., body #1)* on their desks. Students then *travel to a desk of their choice*, taking their **Partner Check** with them. They then fill out the **Partner Check** for the paper at that particular desk.

3. Require that each section be *evaluated by more than one student* so that the author can make a *comparison of his/her peer suggestions.*

Name:__________________Class:__________________Date:______________

Name of Author:____

Partner Check/ Research Rubric #2

1. **List the transition word or phrase that the author uses to introduce the point.**

____

2. **Make an outline of this section.**

____

____

____

____

3. **Rate the job the author is doing in terms of commenting on/interpreting the facts that he/she is presenting.**

Excellent____ Good____ Average____ Below Average____

a. **If the author is doing an excellent or a good job, list the most effective statement that would be considered an analysis of or interpretation of the facts presented.**

____

____

____

b. **If the author is doing more reporting than analysis, show him/her an area that needs attention and write a sentence of your own that could work to tie the factual information to the thesis, thus putting the quotes to use more persuasively.**

1. **Problem:**______________________________________

____

2. **Correction:**______________________________________

____

4. List three particularly well-stated, convincing passages.

a.____

____

b.____

____

c.____

____

5. List three grammatical problems.

a.____

b.______________________________

c.______________________________

6. **What grade would you give this section and why?**

____

____

____

7. **Specifically, state what you feel to be the author's next step and why:**

____

____

____

____

Using Partner Conference for Persuasive Research Paper

1. The **Partner Conference for Persuasive Research Paper** is another variation of a partner rubric. This "check" requires that students mark their partner's papers for **structure** (i.e., thesis statement, key words in topic sentences of body paragraphs, details, best passages, etc.) Also, all problems must be marked on the rough draft of the research paper itself.

2. Require that this **Partner Conference** be done on the final stage in revision with different partners so that the student author can make comparisons in revisionary suggestions.

Name:________________ Class:________________ Date:________________

Partner Conference for Persuasive Research Paper

Author of paper you are reading:________________

Title of paper you are reading:________________

I. Introduction--label the introduction and thesis on your partner's paper.

A, Mark any **particularly good points** on the paper itself.
List two of the best examples:

1.________________

____

2.________________

____

B. Mark any **problems** that you see. What suggestions can you offer?

____

____

II. First aspect--label the first aspect, box in the key word, check mark the details, and mark any particularly cogent points.

A. What is the **point** of this section?

____

____

B. How is it **relevant** to the thesis?

____

____

C. Mark any **problems.** What suggestions can you offer?

____

____

III. Second aspect--label the second aspect, box in the key word, check mark the details, and mark the best parts.

A. What is the **point** of this section?

____

____

B. What makes it **convincing?**

____

____

C. Mark any **problems.** What suggestions can you offer?

____

IV. Third aspect--directions same as above two aspects

A. What is the **point** of this section?

____

____

B. How is it **convincing?**

____

____

C. Mark any **problems.** What suggestions can you offer?

____

____

V. Conclusion--mark the conclusion and the restated thesis.

A. Mark any **attention-getting passages.** List two of the best examples:

1.____

2.____

B. Mark any **problems.** What suggestions can you offer?

____

____

Name:________________ Class:________________ Date:________________

Final Check Sheet for Persuasive Research Paper

All parts of the research paper are **due on**_______________________________.

Papers are to be in this order:

1. Cover Sheet

2. Outline

A. Your outline will have **five Roman numerals** and be a **phrase or topic outline** rather than a sentence outline.

B. Body paragraphs will have **three subdivisions** listed as "A," "B," and "C" and at least **two subpoints** under each letter, which will be listed as "1" and "2."

C. All divisions must be **parallel in structure.**

3. Final Typed Copy of Research Paper

A. Each part of the paper will be typed as **separate parts**; for instance, the first point will not be typed on the same page as the introduction.

B. **Internal footnotes will be color-coded** to correspond to note cards and bibliographic cards used as support, each source representing a different color. Remember to footnote all facts, not just quoted facts.

C. Make appropriate markings on final copy.
   1. Box in key words, the main reason, for each of the three points.
   2. Put a check mark on each detail that supports this point.
   3. Write in the margin: "persuasive summation."

4. Works Cited

A. Be sure to include only those sources that you actually cited in your paper--a minimum of five.

B. Be sure to alphabetize your entries and follow the form given.

C. Entries should be color-coded to correspond to the footnotes in your paper.

5. Note Cards

Note cards will be color-coded, put in the order they appear in the paper, stapled to blank typing paper, and placed after the Works Cited.

6. Rough Copies/Student Response Sheets

All rough copies/response sheets will be included at the end.

Using the Persuasive Reader Response Sheet

1. The purpose of the **Persuasive Reader Response Sheet** is for *class analysis during an oral presentation.* Many curriculums require that students make a presentation each semester, nine-week period, etc.

2. One method of presenting is to require students to make **two final copies** of their research paper, *one from which they read* and *one for the teacher* to use to mark problems, comments, etc. as students present.

3. The class becomes actively involved in the *organization, content, stylistic devices,* etc. of their classmates' papers when they are asked to take notes in the form of the **Persuasive Reader Response Sheet.**

4. After each presentation the teacher may call on students to respond to various questions stated on the **Persuasive Reader Response Sheet**, and a *response grade for each student* can be entered into the grade book at that time. Not only does this provide a daily analysis grade, but the author and the class as a whole can *benefit from comments made by their peers regarding their papers and their manner of presentation.*

Name of Responder: ______________________ Name of Writer: ______________________

Class: ______________________ Date: ______________________

Persuasive Reader Response Sheet

I. Narrative Introduction

A. Explain what you liked about the narrative **introduction**:

____

____

____

B. In your opinion what was the best of the three **aspects/categories** the author used?

1. Category: ______________________

2. Why? ______________________

____

II. *STYLISTIC DEVICES*--List three of the best **sentences/passages**, ones that were particularly descriptive, well-written, etc.

A. ____

B. ____

C. ____

III. FACTS--List three interesting facts the author used:

A. ______________________________

B. ______________________________

C. ______________________________

IV. COMMENTS ABOUT PRESENTATION:

A. ______________________________

B. ______________________________

V. GRADE:

A. What grade would you give the author? ______________

B. Reason: ______________________________

____

Using Research Review and Test

Review for Final Exam

1. **Review for Final Exam** reviews students on the **writing process** (e.g., types, definitions, and examples of prewriting), special **aspects of literary analysis essays** (e.g., using present tense, merging quoted material), and the **research process** (e.g., note card form, Works Cited, internal footnotes).

2. **Review for Final Exam** also includes various **grammatical problems** encountered in the **revision/proofreading stages** (e.g., fragments, run-ons, subject/verb agreement). It asks students to **peruse their portfolio** to ascertain which grammatical mistakes they have most often made. The students must then give the rule for that grammatical concept and show evidence of being able to correct that type of mistake.

Research Test: "In Praise of August"

1. **The Research Test: "In Praise of August"** was designed to test students on their ability to write a **narrative scenario introduction to a proposed research paper** in a classroom setting.

2. Besides the essay test, the **"short answer" section** of the test involves using an article from <u>Time</u> **magazine** as a basis for **synthesizing** their knowledge of research skills.

3. The **article**, which the teacher could run a classroom set, is as follows:

Rosenblatt, Roger. "In Praise of August." <u>Time</u> 26 August 1985: 10-11.

Name:________________________________ **CLASS:**____________ **DATE:**__________

Review for Final Exam

I. Writing Process

A. List, define, and give an example of three types of prewriting:

1.____

____

____

2.____

____

____

3.____

____

____

B. Write a narrative scenario **for a persuasive paper that will do the following:**

1. Set the stage for a proposed persuasive paper
2. Use descriptive/figurative language
3. Avoid the use of first-person singular
4. State the thesis (in active voice) at the end of the scenario

C. Besides narrative, persuasive, and literary analysis papers, list three other types of writing and any "hints" to remember about each.

1. ______________________________

____

2. ______________________________

____

3. ______________________________

____

D. For literary analysis papers list three things you learned:

1. ______________________________

2. ______________________________

3. ______________________________

II. Research Process

A. Note Card Form

1. Define and give an example of a combined note card.

____

____

____

2. **Define and give an example of a** summary note card.

____

____

____

B. Bibliography/Works Cited

Write an entry for an House and Garden (magazine) article entitled "The Return of Gracious Living," written by Louise Pettyjohn, published in June, 1981, and appearing on pages 94-96.

____

____

____

C. Thesis Statement

1. **Define the term** thesis statement: ______________________________

____

____

2. **List and give original examples of** problems to avoid **in thesis statements:**

a. ____

b. ____

c. ____

3. **Write a** thesis statement **for one of your brainstormed persuasive topics.**

____

____

D. Internal Footnotes -- **Write an** internal footnote **for the above magazine article, specifying one page of your choice.**

____

____

III. Revision/Proofreading/Writing Style

A. **Define, give an example of, and correct a** fragment.

1. Definition: ______________________________

____

2. Example: ______________________________

____

3. Correction: ______________________________

____

B. **Define, give an example of, and list the** four ways to correct a run-on sentence.

1. Definition: ______________________________

____

2. Example: ____________________

____

3. Four ways to correct a run-on:

a. ____________ c. ____________

b. ____________ d. ____________

C. **List five ways to** combine sentences for variety.

1. ____________ 4. ____________

2. ____________ 5. ____________

3. ____________

D. **List, define, and give examples of three types of** figurative language devices:

1. ____________________

2. ____________________

3. ____________________

E. **Define and give an example of** repetition for effect.

____

____

____

F. **Define and give an example of** satire.

G. **Define and give an example of** parallel structure.

H. **Choose three** grammatical mistakes **that you have made most often on your papers, write the** rule, **and give an** example of an incorrect sentence and the corrected version.

1. Mistake:
   a. Rule:
   b. Incorrect:
   c. Correct:
2. Mistake:
   a. Rule:
   b. Incorrect:
   c. Correct:
3. Mistake:
   a. Rule:
   b. Incorrect:
   c. Correct:

Answers to:

Review for Final Exam

I. Writing Process

A.

1. **Brainstorming--a quick listing of everything about the topic that just "pops" or "storms" into your brain** (e.g., Topic=Problems in Public Schools: weapons, violence, drugs, discipline, peer pressure, etc.)
2. **Mapping/Webbing/Clustering--like an outline except that main ideas and subpoints are put in circles around the central circle, which is the topic**
3. **Freewriting--writing whatever comes to mind about the topic, but not being concerned about grammatical rules, getting ideas down on paper** (e.g., Problems with public schools include discipline. Involvement with parents. Teachers. Students who fail or have a fear of failure.)

B. Mary walked dejectedly out of the vice-president's office at Fred Banda Enterprises. Her resume had been rejected. She couldn't believe it; she typed 70 words a minute, took shorthand quickly and with few errors, and had even developed her own system of filing. She had always dreamed of a secretarial job, but now it looked like her dreams would remain just that--dreams. Mary got into her car and drove home. At her apartment, she found a letter pushed under her door. "Payment due" it said in bold letters. Mary slumped into a chair. "I was counting on that job," thought Mary. I would have gotten it, too, if it hadn't involved computers. I guess I better get a word processor, some clip-art, and a manual. Mary's plight is similar to that of many people. Technology is a part of lives, but many schools fail to prepare students properly. (Technology should be used in schools because it makes resources available, it can be taught using simple step-by-step procedures, and it can help students be competitive in the job market.) (Tom)-- **Answers will vary.**

C. Answers will vary.

1. **Comparison/Contrast-- use chart with one of the following formulas:**
   A. Similar, similar, different
   B. Different, different, similar
   C. Good, good, bad
   D. Bad, bad, good
   E. Advantage,advantage,disadvantage
   F. Disadvantage, disadvantage, advantage
2. **Description--Base paper on a dominant impression, all the details Supporting this main idea--use a sense web to brainstorm Sights, smells, tastes, touch, and sounds**

3. **Process (how-to)--Steps should be in order and easy for the reader to follow**

D. Other answers could be accepted as well.

1. **Use present tense.**
2. **Blend quoted material with your own words.**
3. **Except for in the thesis, use the author's last name only.**
4. **Identify the text.**
5. **Give attribution for textual material.**

II. Research Process

A.

1. A combined note card summarizes ideas from a source as well as quoting some of the material (e.g., Teachers are being attacked by students--"Each month in secondary schools there are approximately 6,000 teachers robbed, 1,000 teachers assaulted seriously, 125,000 teachers threatened, and 125,000 teachers afraid to administer discipline.")

2. A summary note card condenses material from a source (e.g., Law suits have resulted in teachers attempting discipline.)

B. **Pettyjohn, Louise. "The Return of Gracious Living." House and Garden. June 1981: 94-96.**

C.

1. **The thesis statement is the work's central point.**

2.

a. **Watch out for "announcing" your thesis** (e.g., My paper will discuss the problems of discipline in public schools.)

B. **Make sure the thesis is not too broad** (e.g., Schools have problems.)

C. **Watch out for stating your thesis in an opinionated manner** (e.g., Schools have problems in discipline due to children who are losers, lazy teachers, and ineffective administrators.)

3. **People should include fine arts as a regular part of their lives because of the therapeutic benefits inherent in art, music, and dance.**

4. **(Pettyjohn 96)**

III. Revision/Proofreading/Writing Style

A. Answers will vary.

1. **A fragment is an incomplete sentence.**
2. **Walking down the street in my new clothes.**
3. **Walking down the street in my new clothes, I noticed the admiring glances.**

B.

1. **A run-on sentence is two or more sentences not properly combined.**
2. **I like you, you like me.**
3.
   - **A. Period**
   - **B. Semicolon**
   - **C. Comma and conjunction**
   - **D. Clause signal (since, because, if, etc.)**

C. Answers will vary.

1. **Compound sentence**
2. **Complex sentence**
3. **Compound/complex sentence**
4. **Compound parts (e.g., verbs, direct objects, etc.)**
5. **Appositives**

D. Answers will vary.

1. **Simile--a comparison between two unlike things using "like" or "as"** (e.g., Her hair is like seaweed.)
2. **Metaphor--a comparison between two unlike things not using "like" or "as"** (e.g., "All the world is a stage.")

3. Personification--giving human traits to something not human
(e.g., The willow branches bent down and kissed the earth.)

E. Repetition for effect is repeating words to create a poetic or persuasive effect
(e.g., It is mothers who give us our sense of the world. It is mothers who make us laugh or cry. It is mothers who mend all broken hearts.)

F. Satire is poking fun at a situation, a person, etc. (e.g., Riding in a cab in any major city could be considered on the same scale as any other major crime: assault and battery (our bodies as well as our senses are assaulted and battered), robbery (we're often robbed of our theory of good will toward men), and kidnaping (surely there is a ransom and a high-speed chase) involved.)

G. Parallel structure is placing words or phrases in similar grammatical structure
(e.g. nouns with nouns, verb phrases with verb phrases, etc.)
(e.g., I like sailing, swimming, and surfing--all -ing verbs.)

H. Answers will vary.

Name:______________________Class:______________Date:____________

Research Test "In Praise of August"

I. **Essay**--You may **not refer to any books or notes** for this section of the test; this does not, however, include a **dictionary**, which you might need for the proofreading of your essay. **You will hand in this section** (with this assignment sheet) before picking up the second section of your exam.

A. **Narrative Scenario**--Write a **rough draft introduction** of at least **200 words** (count the total number of words and place on the bottom of your final draft) for a **persuasive/argumentative research paper** whose thesis deals with **praising the month of August**.

1. Development: The paper itself, which you will obviously not write, could be developed in a number of ways, one of which might be the following:

A. Introduction
b. Important political events that occurred in the U.S. during the month of August
c. Important political events that occurred outside the US during the month of August
d. Frivolous/humorous events that occurred during the month of August
e. Conclusion

2. Purpose of Introduction: Whatever the body of the paper could be, whatever the plan of development--which you will include in your thesis statement in your introduction--the introduction could simply be an attention-getter, one that gets the reader thinking about your topic. Make sure that your introduction could lead to a paper whose aspects could be researched.

3. Prewriting: You might want to simply describe what August is like; therefore a sense web might result in useful images. You could brainstorm activities that happen in August--baseball games, lazy afternoons, etc. Keep in mind that the entire point is to interest readers in the month of August.

B. Final draft of narrative scenario--After revising and proofreading, write a final draft that includes your total word count.

Rubric:

1. Fragments (unless labeled for effect)
2. Run Ons
3. Spelling
4. Other grammatical concerns (subject/verb agreement, etc.)
5. Point of view
6. Stylistic devices (figurative language, repetition for effect, etc.)
7. Clear thesis statement and plan of development

II. Short Answer--Now that you have written your narrative scenario introduction praising the month of August, read the article in Time entitled "In Praise of August," which could be viewed as a persuasive/argumentative research paper of sorts with a descriptive introduction. Using the article itself, answer the following questions that involve aspects of the writing/research process.

A. Note Cards

1. Take one "combined" note card on one important event of a serious nature that occurred during the month of August.

2. Take one summary note card listing five frivolous/humorous events that occurred during August. (Note: list the events.)

B. Bibliography/Works Cited--Write a bibliographic entry for this article, paying special attention to all punctuation.

___

___

C. Quoted material as substantiation of thesis and blending of quoted material--If you were writing a research paper arguing the importance of the month of August, you might wish to use indisputable facts gathered from various sources (as the author of this article obviously has done) and you might want to quote someone's opinion that aligns itself with you own, thus giving your views even more weight. One point you might want to argue in a research paper of this nature--besides serious events and happenings of a lighter nature--is the philosophical/aesthetic nature of the month.

1. Make a statement of your own about the special beauty of the month and quote a brief passage from the article that would serve as support for your own ideas.

___

___

___

2. Write an internal footnote to document your quote. (For the author, use the first author listed in the byline.)

___

D. Stylistic Devices:

1. **Repetition for effect**--We have learned to use repetition for effect. Explain the **author's repeated use of "not"** in the introductory paragraph. In other words, **what effect do you think he is trying to create?**

____

____

____.

2. Quote a **simile** from the conclusion and **explain its effect:**

____

____

____

3. Quote a **personification** from the conclusion and **explain its effect:**

____

____

____

F. Grammatical Aspects

A. **Fragments**--We have talked about the **intentional use of fragments--fragments for effect.**

1. Quote a **fragment from this article** (besides the one referred to in Part D of this test.)

____

2. Specifically **explain the effect** of this particular fragment on the reader.

____

____

3. **Correct the fragment** by adding to it or by combining it with the sentence before or after.

____

____

B. Run On--Correct the following run-on sentence using all four **methods** we have discussed.

Run On: August is no fool, it knows its limitations.

1.____
2.____
3.____
4.____

PART IV

COMPARISON/ CONTRAST RESEARCH

Using Illustrator and Author

1. The **Illustrator and Author** assignment was designed to be used in conjunction with a **comparison/contrast writing unit.**

2. Require that students complete the assignment on an **in-class novel** or an **independent reading book.**

3. Students enjoy using their **artistic talents** (or their expertise at computer graphics) and designing a **unique cover.**

4. Classes may wish to present their book covers and paper in a **"book talk,"** interesting students in their library books.

5. Hold **contests** for the best essay and cover.

Name:________________________ class:______________ Date:______________

Illustrator and Author

Assignment:

Design a book jacket for your book. Your purpose is to introduce the book through comparing and contrasting two characters, two situations, etc.

Example:

☞ **For instance, Margaret Atwood for her novel** Cat's Eye **might have chosen to entice readers by writing:**

Meet Elaine and Cordelia, childhood friends of the early '50's, who share their love for boys and a rebellious attitude but who ultimately differ in what it means to be friends.

☞ **While you must give** specific details **to sell the book, you must be somewhat mysterious so as to not give away the entire plot.**

☞ **You may use your** comparison/contrast chart**, which must include at least three details per category.**

☞ **The** rubric and paper must be done **in class; however, you will design the product** (the book jacket) **for a separate grade at home.**

Remember:

1. **An author can reveal** characterization **in six ways.**

   A. Appearance
   B. Actions
   C. Speech
   D. Environment
   E. Inner thoughts and feelings
   F. What others say about him/her

2. **Write about literature in** present tense.
3. Underline **book titles.**
4. Proofreading **is essential. Remember to** blend quoted material **from the text with your own words.**

Monica Prince
Library Book Test
Illustrator and Author

Out of Phase

Let's visit Phase and Proton, two very different frames, that are different in appearance and personality, but similar in the happiness of their inhabitants. We'll discover the differences of science and magic.

To begin with, the appearance of Proton and Phase are as different as the proverbial night and day. Comparing the "open chambers" (45) in Proton to the "open, grassy plains" (50) of Phase is like comparing the sun to the moon. The literally living woods, prisoners to the Adepts, or magic wielders, do help shelter Phase's many little creatures. Also, the creatures are very different in the two frames. The animal-heads and unicorns are abundant in Phase, but only humans, aliens, androids, and robots live in Proton. The humanoid robots of Proton live in domes so that the polluted air from outside won't kill them. In Phase, however, the sky is as blue as the clearest lake waters on Earth.

In addition to being totally different in appearances, Phase and Proton's personalities vary. In Proton, the "self-willed machines" (41) help people, but in Phase, the unicorns protect people. So, as we can clearly see, the basis of Phase is magic, whereas Proton thrives on science. Without magic or science, the frames would be equal and would destroy each other because of the imbalance created. The population of the frames differs also. The overpopulated domes of Proton are full and busy, but Phase, with its green lands and hardly a living soul on it, is very different. Most of Phase's creatures stick to the forests and are in limited supply, unlike citizens and aliens of Proton. The noisiness of the frames is very different as well. In Phase, all that is heard is the whispering of the cool breeze and birds cawing in the distance, unlike Proton's noises of motor vehicles and oxygen pumps. They are, actually, as different as black and white.

Even though Phase and Proton are so different in personality and appearance, they are similar in the happiness of their people. Both frames have something to entertain their inhabitants. In Phase, it is magic. As the Translucent Adept says, "I enchanted this boat to float on air, that's all" (2). In Proton, the entertainment is the Journey, a tournament between serfs and/or citizens, where the winner is granted citizenship. It is made up of "grids" where one person "has numbers" and one person "has letters" (88). Also in both frames, the people love it where they are. Phase's people love the beautiful woods and clear blue skies, and Proton's people love its machines, domes, and polluted environment. Each frame has people that have more rights than the others, and those people seem to be in control. The Citizens and Adepts, who act like kings and queens, think that they rule all, but a lot goes on that they don't know about.

So, as we can see, Phase and Proton are two totally different places, but they do have similarities. There are differences in their appearances **and** personalities **but similarities in the** happiness**, which makes them two different frames with their own ways.**

How to Write a Comparison/Contrast Research Paper

1. Students should **brainstorm topics** in which they are interested, making sure that these topics can be researched. **Or** teachers may prefer that students choose from a list of **teacher-chosen topics**.

2. Next, ask students to do a **Write to Learn**, listing as many **facts** as possible that they already know as well as **questions** regarding information that they need to find through research.

3. Then ask students to complete a **comparison/contrast chart** in terms of *topics, categories, and formula*, explaining to them that the details will be filled in with researched information.

4. Require that a certain number of **note cards** *(e.g., at least ten per aspect/category)* be completed each library period. **Check note cards** for *form, plagiarism, pertinent information, etc.*

5. After the initial research has been done, students may then do a **final Write to Learn**, which will indicate to them what they have now learned and where any **"holes" in the research** still exist.

6. In class, students should **divide note cards** into aspects and **write one aspect per period/day, etc.**

7. Students might need to **discuss the intention/purpose/plan** for each aspect with a partner before actually beginning the writing process. The **partner's questions/feedback** could give the student-author tips to guide him/her through the initial stages.

8. Remind students that all researched information must be **documented**, whether it is quoted or paraphrased.

9. Use **partner checks, row checks, or Musical Chairs** for each aspect so that the student-author can better assess his/her progress.

10. The **Structure Rubric** should be used so that students are certain to have the necessary **format.**

11. Ask students to **highlight quoted or paraphrased information** to make sure that the researched facts are blended with the students' own words and to form a visual image for the student of the amount of research versus the student's own words.

Laura Reid/6th grade

Comparison/Contrast

Research Paper

China Vs. America

Lin walked quietly down the halls of the White House, listening to every word of the tour guide, observing the rooms and pictures. In the lobby she had seen lots of books on the government. And in the zoo, information on wildlife. When she was back in Williamsburg, she had seen a lot of material on the local architecture. Everything in America was so different from things in China. America was like a space-aged movie. Americans were so much more modernized, it seemed. Lin knew a six-week, heaven-made vacation was not long enough to learn everything about America that she yearned to uncover. But it would have to do for the time being. She would have to be a roadrunner speeding through places, sucking up information, and storing it.

Lin was surprised at the zoo when she learned how different its wildlife was. For instance, some of America's remaining animals--the beaver, fox, mink, muskrat, possum, and coon--live in rivers and trees that cover one-third of the land in America (Gunther 69). Countless varieties of fish occupy the flowing waters that creep their way through the land (Gunther 69). Lin thought how exotic those animals looked and felt. In contrast, she thought about some of China's animals, the Giant Panda, the Golden Monkey, and the tiger (Chen 390). She thought about all the cypress, pine, and bamboo that covered her homeland (Chen 390). Thoughts drifted in about all the species of plants in China and how some of them date back all the way to the Ice Age, untouched (Chen 390). She longed to be in her cozy little home. The thought of it made her wonder, "What would it be like to come home to a house here, a long time ago?"

The Tourist Information Center buzzed with tourists from all corners of the world. Lin picked up a book, slowly absorbing the information printed out in front of her. She read how the American early settlers cut their own wood for their homes (Kalman 8). At the beginning they built small, one-story, one-room houses (Kalman 9). On the next page Lin learned about later on in America. When the communities grew and became more populated, the houses grew as well and people began to make two-story homes for their families (Kalman 9). Lin sat down on a nearby bench and began to dream of her home in China. She remembered her teacher saying, "'Chinese architects were the first to design buildings to fit into natural settings'" (Chen 380). Pictures formed in her mind. In China, there are one-story buildings sitting on the land, but right next to them are tall buildings called Pagodas (Dernberger 490). Their buildings were also constructed of wood, but were sometimes built with stone with soft tile ceilings (Dernberger 490) that sounded musical in the rain, like a sort of lullaby.

Finally, the tour was over! Lin's parents, just like always, were talking to the guide so she sat down on a chair and thought again about what she had learned before the tour. Just like in China, there is a President, except America's President is in charge of the executive branch (Carleton 77), and China's is in charge of the Republic of China (Chen 378). They also both have a Vice-President. The Chinese Vice-President attends formal conferences and parties (Chen 378). The American Vice-President is presiding officer of the U.S. Senate and if something should happen to the President, he will take over (Carleton 77). Both countries have an armed forces group. China has the C.M.A. headed by a chairman and consisting of the P.L.A., A.P.F. and the militia (Chen 378), whereas America has the Department of Defense, which includes the Marine Corps, Coast Guard, Army, Air Force, and Navy (Carleton 79). As she looked at her parents still talking to the guide, she wondered if they felt, as she did, that American and China might not be so different after all.

Yes, the countries are different, and the wildlife difference surprised Lin. She thought of how weird and freaky some of those animals looked and felt. She imagined the tall Pagodas and the small wooden cabins she had seen in a book about

the log houses. Here inside the walls of the White House, Lin discovered how alike the governments are with both a President and Vice-President. How exciting it would be to go home and tell her friends about what she had learned and what she has yet to discover.

Name:______________________ Class:________________ Date:_________________

Comparison/Contrast Research Rubric #1 Organization & Research Material

I. **Narrative scenario introduction & conclusion:**

Explain the purpose of your narrative scenario introduction and conclusion.

____

____

____

____

II. **Write to Learn:**

For each aspect of your paper, state the formula (SSD; DDS; AAD; DDA; GGB; BBG) and category, then explain what each aspect tries to accomplish.

A. Aspect #1: ________ (formula); _______________ (category)

Explanation:____

____

____

B. Aspect #2:_______ (formula); ______________ (category)

Explanation: ____

____

____

C. Aspect #3:_______ (formula); ______________ (category)

Explanation: ____

____

____

III. Footnotes for paraphrased information:

Cite an example from your paper of a sentence that contains an internal footnote for paraphrased information. Include the footnote along with the sentence. Remember that the PERIOD goes after the parentheses.

____

____

____

IV. Footnotes for quoted information:

Cite an example from your paper of a sentence that contains an internal footnote for quoted material. Remember to introduce the quote with words of your own. The sentence should sound smooth--a blending of your own words with carefully selected quoted material.

____

____

____

Name:____________________Class:____________________Date:______________

Comparison/Contrast Research Rubric #2 Revision

1. For all three aspects, explain in your own words how at least three paraphrased/quoted references help make your point.

A. Aspect #1

1.____

____

____

2.____

____

____

3.____

____

____

B. Aspect #2

1.____

____

Comparison/Contrast Research Rubric #2: Revision

2. ______

3. ______

C. Aspect #3

1. ______

2. ______

3. ______

II. Based on your work on the question above, explain **how you could revise an aspect** to make it **more effective.**

____

____

____

III. Give three examples of how you **revised sentences** to contain the following **sophisticated sentence structures.**

A. Noun Absolute: (NOUN FOLLOWED BY A PRESENT OR PAST PARTICIPLE--E.G., MY KNEES SHAKING, I WALKED INTO THE OFFICE. MY GLASSES LOWERED, I LOOKED AT HIM ACROSS THE DESK.)

____

____

B. PARTICIPIAL PHRASE: (AN -ING WORD GROUP THAT WORKS AS AN ADJECTIVE TO MODIFY AN NOUN--E.G., RUNNING INTO THE GRAMMATICAL PROBLEM AGAIN, I DECIDED TO RECAST THE SENTENCE ENTIRELY.)

____

____

C. UNUSUAL/INVERTED ORDER: (any order that does not follow the "standard" subject/verb pattern)

____

____

Name:__________________________Class:______________Date:_______________

Comparison/Contrast Research Rubric #3 Proofreading

I. Transition Words:

For your **first aspect**, give examples of transition words/phrases that you used to signal the reader that a subpoint is being made:

a.________________________________

b.________________________________

c.________________________________

II. Run-Ons:

For your **second aspect**, cite an example of how you avoided a run-on sentence.

____

____

III. Fragments:

For your **third aspect**, cite an example of how you avoided a fragment.

____

____

IV. Spelling: List five words that you spell-checked:

a. ______________________________

B. ______________________________

C. ______________________________

D. ______________________________

E. ______________________________

V. Other Grammatical Errors: Using your other graded essays, cite two specific errors other than the ones mention above and explain how you have proofread for these:

A. Error #1: ______________________

EXPLANATION: ____

____

____

B. ERROR #2: ______________________

EXPLANATION: ____

____

____

Name of Responder:____________________ Name of Writer:________________

Response Sheet for Comparison/Contrast

I. **Narrative Scenario Introduction & Conclusion**--Explain how the scenarios helped make the author's point or how they could have been improved.

____

____

____

II. **Best Aspect**--In your opinion, what was the best of the three aspects (TOPICS/CATEGORIES) the author used in comparing and contrasting.

A. Category:______________________________

B. Explanation:______________________________

____

III. **Interesting Facts**--List three interesting facts the author used:

A.____

B.____

C.____

IV. Grammatical/Proofreading Errors--Cite any grammatical/proofreading errors the author made:

A.____

B.____

C.____

V. Revision--Explain what you feel to be the weakest point of the paper and give suggestions for revision:

A. Weakness:____________________________________

____

B. Suggestions:__________________________________

____

____

____

VI. Rating--Overall, how would you rate this paper and why?

A. Rating:____________________________

B. Explanation:___________________________________

____

____

PART V

Descriptive Research

How to Use Methods of Elaboration

1. Using their **library book or class novel**, students should **cite examples** of the following **Methods of Elaboration**. Remind students of the necessity of using *internal footnotes, quotes within quotes, etc.* when applicable.

2. **Use the Methods of Elaboration** sheet as a **rubric** to reinforce the usage of various methods of **support/detail** within an essay. Require that students cite a certain number of examples from their papers to **prove the inclusion** of these types of elaboration.

3. The following are **student-written examples** of the various methods of elaboration.

Methods of Elaboration

1. **Action Verbs:** He could jam; he could slam. He could do the whimmy wham....They were shooting and spinning, whooping and juicing, slamming and jamming ....(Ardi)

2. **Adjectives/Adverbs:**

   Adjectives: I led a great army over the knee-high weeds, over the dead animal carcasses, and over the dangerous, to-be-avoided ant hills.(Ryan)

   Adverbs: You strike as quickly as a King Cobra but as quietly as a mouse. (Angela)

3. **Allusions:** The fantasy luxuries depicted on the cartoon "The Jetsons," combined with very real ones reserved for stars of "The Lifestyles of the Rich and Famous," pale in comparison to those in our own private dream worlds. (Mary)

4. **Analogies:** A number of similarities exists between life and a roller coaster. The journey starts out innocently enough as we find ourselves standing in line for the roller coaster. After we board, we are locked in snug and tight. Secure as a newborn baby wrapped in swaddling cloth, we have no idea of what's ahead. Then it begins--that palm-sweating, gut-wrenching, butterflies-flying feeling in the pit of our stomachs as anxious anticipation builds while waiting, waiting for the ride to begin. (Karen)

5. **Anecdotes:** And, oh, how we loved the blackberry cobbler. One day out of the summer, Mother would send us on a blackberry harvest. Armed only with buckets from recent visits to McDonalds, we trooped out into our own world. It was like a contest....Our little hunt lasted from after "Sesame Street" was over to when the "Muppet Show" was due to air. (Teri)

6. **Definitions:** Utopia...a place with dragons soaring at unimaginable heights, with wizards casting spells, and elfin archers saving people with the earth so filled with magic. (Tom)

7. **Descriptions:** Gone will be the monotony of neighborhoods we're used to, where each house resembles the next except for a curlicue here and a doodad there, and in its place will be winding, red-bricked streets and rainbow-colored houses, some with gables and dormer windows, rooftop decks, and tri-level porches. (Mary)

8. **Dialogue:** As I walk into the kitchen, I see a ham sandwich on the table with a note that says, "I love you! From your mother." I then realize that everybody loves me. That is what is right about my life. (Helmuth)

9. **Examples/Explanations/Illustrations:** One of the things that we like best about Carlsbad Caverns is the sights...lots of unique formations underground, such as totem poles, stalagmites, and rock draperies. (Doug)

10. **Facts:** According to Michael Samuels in "Art as a Healing Force," a number of doctors use art to diagnose and treat their patients....(which includes) teaching people to use art for growth and healing purposes....(including) the treatment of various diseases such as cancer, AIDS, and heart disease. (Melissa)

11. **Figurative Language:** In those woods, I would spend hours listening to the wind rustle the leaves, climbing trees and spying on nesting birds, and giving the occasional wild growl to scare away any pink-flowered girls who might be riding their bikes too close to my secret entrance. (Todd)

12. **Quotations:** I was a little girl with rosy-red cheeks, always bearing a smile on my face, a twinkle in my eye, and an imaginative mind on the lookout for adventure. I guess I always knew what Albert Einstein once said was true: "Imagination is more important than knowledge." (Tiffany)

13. **Reasons:** When you think of my name, you think innocence and that's why I say it hides me. I have come to like this label maybe because it raised me. I get lost in thoughts of it, so thick I feel blind. Maybe if you could slice through it all, you could see me, but you never will, for I haven't decided what I am. I'm not yet registered as a person. (Joey)

14. **Sensory Images:** Originally, my father was going to name me Deequeta, a pins-and-needles name. Like chili pepper and crispy chips, a tangy swing to it. But my beef-iron-and-wine mother wouldn't hear of such a name. (Julie)

15. **Other:**

How to Use Library Book Test Descriptive Mode

1. The **Library Book Test** was designed to be used in conjunction with a **descriptive writing unit.**

2. The assignment reinforces all stages of the **writing process** in that it asks students to prewrite--brainstorm three memorable scenes from their book and make a web using quoted material from the text--compose a rough draft, proofread and revise, and reshape into a final version.

3. Students are reviewed on such **literary analysis skills** as combining quoted material with the student-writer's own work, incorporating internal footnotes, and using present tense verbs.

4. Classes enjoy the different format, namely that of a **memo** to a production supervisor.

Name:______________________________ Class:______________ Date:____________

Library Book Test Descriptive Mode

Situation:

The World Premiere of ______________________________ (write the name of your book) **is being presented by Theater Under the Stars and will open at the Wortham in Houston.**

As the producer, you must write a memo to the production supervisors **and technicians,** describing all the scenes **as you envision them from the script. Of course, there could be many settings, but to begin with you must give them** one main setting **on which to concentrate their efforts.**

Process of completion of task:

In order to decide on the scene you'd like for them to begin with, brainstorm **three possible scenes portrayed in the text:**

1. ____
2. ____
3. ____

Web:

After your brainstorming, pick one scene that you think you can describe accurately using your own interpretation of the script **as well as** quoted material **from the text itself.**

To do this, web three aspects **of that scene that must be portrayed for the audience to understand the author's intent.**

Rubric:

1. Accuracy of quote incorporation **in literary analysis:**

a. Quotes must be introduced with your own words; quoted material cannot stand alone. Avoid creating run-ons when merging your words with the author's.

b. An internal footnote, which consists of the page number in parentheses, must follow every quote.

c. Remember not to plagiarize. All words must be your own except for the words you choose to quote.

2. Tense--**Use** present tense **for literary analysis.**

3. Structure--**Write a** five-paragraph descriptive essay **with a** dominant impression supported by three places, **one quote per place.**

Example:

To: J. Harris
From: Teacher Sample
Date: 12/3/97
Re: Technical aspects of "Memories of Christmas"

As the worker of technical miracles, you will be relieved that we're starting with one scene in our portrayal of Dylan Thomas's "Memories of Christmas," namely that of the old forbidding house where the narrator and his friends go Christmas caroling on Christmas Eve. Since we will want the audience to experience the fear the young boys have approaching this dark, ominous place, special attention should be paid to every aspect of its staging.

First, Thomas describes the night as being so completely black that "there wasn't the shaving of a moon to light the secret, white-flying streets" (5), which means that you will have a special challenge on your hands, making plenty of swirling snow visible against this ebony background.

Besides the eeriness of the night, the sound effects must be convincing. As the boys make their way up the drive, the audience must hear the very sounds the boys hear, ones that conjure up nightmarish visions perhaps of "web-footed men wheezing in caves" (5). Wind whipping through tree branches and howling like a vicious animal on the prowl will generate suspense that will lead effectively to the climax.

Finally, the voice of the old man behind the door requires a special touch. After the boys reach the house and begin to sing, a voice behind closed doors feebly tries to accompany them. Since this is a house of mystery, the voice must be a voice of mystery as well. Thomas describes "a small, dry voice (coming) through the keyhole" sounding "like the voice of someone who has not spoken for a long time" (5). The quality of the voice must be

frightening enough to continue the author's intended tone of the story yet somewhat frail and feeble in order to produce a sort of heartwarming effect on the audience. They must hear in that faceless sound the voice of someone who has decided to reenter humanity if only until the end of a song.

Bob, I have full confidence in your ability to create the necessary special effects of the snowy night, the driveway sounds, and the voice. **Thanks to you, the story will live in the minds of our audience for years to come.**

Liz Alexander
Library Book Test
Descriptive Mode (Memo Form)
The Wizard of Oz

The Wizard of Oz

To: Jay Harris
From Liz Alexander
Date: 12/2/98
Re: Technical aspects of The Wizard of Oz

Knowing that special effects can either break or make the show, I think that you need to pay special attention to the "Dainty China Country" scene. The audience needs to feel that what they are seeing is real so that the magical, jolly mood of the story is maintained. There are many parts of this scene that require "technical miracles."

First of all, there needs to be a huge, high wall that seems "...to be made of white china (and is)...smooth, like the surface of a dish" (184). When making such a wall, you need to keep in mind that Dorothy and her friends will have to cross it by means of a ladder made by the Tin Woodman. You also need to consider that the wall needs to be sturdy and wide enough that they can sit on it. Be sure to make it look like glass.

An even bigger problem is that when Dorothy and her friends go over the wall, all the people living on the other side are "...all made of China, even to their clothes" (187). You will probably need to hire a choreographer to make the rainbow-painted people's movements stiff, as if truly they are people made of glass. Also, Dorothy spooks a cow, who then breaks his porcelain leg. This must not be scary or gory, for this often happens in this country, and a milkmaid simply has to take him to the mender's shop.

Finally, you must consider that the people are "...so small that the tallest of them was no higher than Dorothy's knee" (187). Everything in this country is very small, but perhaps you could use some special lighting to make Dorothy look big. You will need to make the trees, houses, and buildings all appear smaller than Dorothy. These things need to seem so dainty that a small sneeze would make them fall over, which--in fact--does.

Jay, I have total faith in you and that you can successfully complete these special effects. I'm sure you will find some way to make the glass wall, create people who look like china, and devise a way to make everything look small.

How to Use "My Best Friend..." and Analysis

1. "My Best Friend and Those Saturday Mornings" is a sample of a student-written narrative whose strengths lie in its descriptive passages. It is important for students to realize that modes of writing do not exist in isolation, that they include other modes as well (E.G., A NARRATIVE THAT USES DESCRIPTION TO MAKE A POINT).

2. Students can review the elements of a narrative and the use of description as a Method of Elaboration.

3. The "Analysis" provides students with an opportunity to research various aspects of the paper, giving them practice not only in the research process itself but also in using the information in a paper.

4. The "Analysis" also requires that students analyze stylistic devices/methods of elaboration such as MAGIC 3's, IMAGERY, VIVID VERBS, FIGURATIVE LANGUAGE, ETC.

Jerad Norris
Descriptive/Narrative
Model for Library Research
Winner of Harris County"Best Young Writers" Award

My Best Friend and Those Saturday Mornings

I was in deep sleep and having the best dream. Suddenly a hand violently shook my body. My eyes opened fast, and laughter floated in the air. "I got you!" Travis wailed.

"Shut up and let me get dressed," I said calmly pretending not to be startled. Every Saturday at 5:30 a.m., my best friend Travis and I would go fishing at some river. He called it "our river" because we had supposedly claimed it ours back in 1967. Nobody ever walked even near it. I asked a group of adults one day over near the General Store why nobody ever went down there, and they said because it smells like...and I not supposed to say the other word.

I shook the memory out of my head before Travis slapped me and told me to snap out of it. I scanned, searched, and traced the floor for some decent-smelling clothes. I kept all my clothes on the floor because I don't believe in closets. I fell out of bed and gathered some clothes together that were bunched in the corner. A gray shirt, some shorts, and two socks that were different colors and size. I straightened the sheets a little bit and called my morning chore of making my bed good. I pulled my hair down with my fingers and washed my face with some water that had gathered on my window sill. I slipped on some grass-stained Nike shoes that were too little and hurt my big toe.

Travis, on the other hand, was quite different from me. He was known far and wide for his neatness, but not for his behavior. He would wake up and make his bed up perfectly. You wouldn't find a ruffle or crease anywhere. He would pick clothes out that would suit a king from a closet as big as my room. He would brush his teeth till they had a glare on them. His hair, a vast pasture of smooth silk, and not one hair was out of place. His behavior, however, was enough to make his parents yell out that they hate kids and they were never going to have another one. He was known across the country for his spitballs and fists. He had a longer criminal record than any of the most notorious villains. He had more probations and mug shots than serial killers. And yet, he was my best friend.

Then as I was about to go on to another thought, a hand came across my face. "Hey, snap out of it and let's go," Travis marveled in his I'm-in-control voice. I didn't say anything.

I walked outside and grasped my bamboo fishing rod that has been fished with since my great, great, great, great-grandfather, or something like that. The tip was rotting off, and yet the hook lay still, perfect in shape, just calling for a fish. In all the four years Travis and I had fished at that river, we had never caught one fish...not even a mullet. We just went down there to waste time till the double feature came on at the movies for only a nickel.

"Hey, snap out of it and let's go!" Travis yelled in an exasperated voice.

I took a step.

"Last one there wears his mama's bra," Travis shouted.

I took off at full speed, stopping at nothing because if I lost I would be made fun of at school for the kid that wears his mama's bra. Travis was beating me at what seemed like a million miles distance between him and me. Running as fast as I could, I tripped on a root that bulged out of the ground lying in wait for an unsuspecting foot. It was big, brown, and it was right in the middle of the driest dirt road in Texas. I landed in the dirt, and a cloud of dust circled around my body. My head lifted, I saw Travis' hand reach out to mine. I grabbed onto it, and he helped me up. "You all right?"

"Yeah, let's finish the race," I said. Believe it or not, he let me win, but he said he didn't. I knew the truth.

The year was 1971 that I realized that Travis was my best friend. We fished all that morning, and around noon Travis whispered in my ear, "Let's go to the double feature now, and it's on me...I'll pay the whole nickel."

Name:______________________ Class:__________________ Date:__________________

Analysis of "My Best Friend and Those Saturday Mornings"

1. Research--Using the model "My Best Friend and Those Saturday Mornings," research the following aspects from the story and write a version of that passage that includes the researched information.

☺ Remember that the idea is to enhance the paper with factual inclusions woven in unobtrusively with the text.

☺ Be sure to include internal footnotes (AUTHOR'S LAST NAME AND PAGE NUMBERS) for facts.

☺ Remember also that footnoted information cannot be common knowledge.

A. 1967--(Here you could "ground" the reader in the setting more by perhaps giving some events from that year in the form of a "magic three." The rewrite could read something along the line of "1967, the year..., ..., and ....)

1. Fact:____

____

____

2. Bibliographic entry: ______________________________

____

3. Rewrite of passage: ______________________________

____

____

B. Notorious villains--

(Here you could not only list "villains'" names but what crime they were famous for as well, making the metaphoric comparison the author uses between his friend and these criminals even more humorous.)

1. Fact: ______________________________

____

____

2. Bibliographic entry: ______________________________

____

3. Rewrite of passage: ______________________________

____

____

C. Types of fish/bait, etc.--

(For this research, you could look up anything regarding fishing--fish, bait--to give the passage more detail. The rewrite could be that these boys hadn't caught a ...or...or..., and they had used...and...and..., and not even a mullet was interested.)

1. Fact: ____________________

____

____

2. Bibliographic entry: ____________________

____

3. Rewrite of passage: ____________________

____

____

D. Movies of 1971-- (You'll have to be careful to make the type of movie fit the story in that the double feature would have to be appropriate for two young boys on a Saturday afternoon.)

1. Fact: ____________________

____

____

2. Bibliographic entry: ____________________

____

3. Rewrite of passage: ____________________

____

____

2. Analysis--in order to be able to write an interesting, well-written paper, student writers can benefit from analyzing aspects of model papers.

✏ Quote an example for each of the following from "My Best Friend...."

A. Magic 3: ______________________________

____

B. Imagery: ______________________________

____

C. Three vivid verbs: __________, __________, __________

D. Two metaphors:

1. ______________________________

2. ______________________________

E. Two specific details for effect:

1. ______________________________

2. ______________________________

F. Hyperbole: ______________________________

G. Personification: ______________________________

H. Humor: ______________________________

I. Hyphenated Modifier: ______________________________

How to Use Smiley-Face Tricks

1. Students can keep **Smiley-Face Tricks** in their binders/notebooks all year as a reminder of various **stylistic devices.**

2. Require that students incorporate a certain number of **Smiley-Face Tricks** in each **essay**, labeling the devices in the margin of their paper.

3. Ask students to use the **Smiley-Face Chart** to cite examples of each **Smiley-Face Trick** from their in-class short stories/novels or their independent reading books.

Smiley-Face Tricks

1. Magic 3--Three examples in a series can create a poetic rhythm or at least add support for a point, especially when the three items have their own modifiers.

"In those woods, I would spend hours **listening** to the wind rustle the leaves, **climbing** trees and spying on nesting birds, and **giving** the occasional wild growl to scare away any pink-flowered girls who might be riding their bikes too close to my secret entrance." (Todd, college freshman)

2. Figurative Language--Non-literal comparisons--such as similes, metaphors, and personification--add "spice" to writing and can help paint a more vivid picture for the reader.

Street, I didn't like it. My room was hot, cramped, and **stuffy as a train in the middle of the Sahara.** And the **looming skeleton-like gray and white frame** of the place scared me. I dared not imagine living there, but the backyard, oh, the

backyard. It was a huge, long mass of plentifully growing trees and blackberries. Goodness, how I loved them." (Teri, grade 7)

3. Specific Details for Effect--Instead of general, vague descriptions, specific sensory details help the reader visualize the person, place, thing, or idea that you are describing.

"It's one of those experiences where you want to **call a radio station** and tell your problems to **some guy who calls himself Dr. Myke**, but who isn't more of a doctor than your pet hamster is, one of those experiences where you want to **read a sappy Harlequin novel** and **listen to Barry Manilow** with a box of bonbons as your best friend, one of those experiences where you wouldn't be surprised if someone came up to you and asked **exactly what time yesterday you were born**. Yeah, one of those." (Ileana, Grade 7)

"Remember the time I worked all day Saturday on an English paper? Sunday I accidentally left the only copy I had at your house. You politely handed it back to me the next day, first period, when it was due. But all over page one you'd drawn **zombies**; page two contained **detailed pictures of yet-to-be-discovered worms**; page three was **visited by various space aliens**; the fourth page **featured scenes from Australia and Florida**; and the last page was **covered with 'Mr. Jenkins is a dork,' 'English stinks,'**

and 'Mr. Jenkins is a four-eyed geek.' Maybe that's why he gave me a D-."
(Liz, grade 8)

4. Repetition for effect--Writers often repeat specially chosen words or phrases to make a point, to stress certain ideas for the reader.

"The veranda is your only shelter **away from** the sister in bed asleep, **away from** the brother that plays in the treehouse in the field, **away from** your chores that await you." (Leslie, grade 7)

5. Expanded Moment--Instead of "speeding" past a moment, writers often emphasize it by "expanding" the actions.

"But no, I had to go to school. And as I said before, I had to listen to my math teacher preach about numbers and letters and figures....I was tired of hearing her annoying voice lecture about 'a=b divided by x.' I glared at the small black hands on the clock, silently threatening them to go faster. But they didn't listen, and I caught myself wishing I were on white sand and looking down at almost transparent pale-blue water with Josh at my side....I don't belong in some dumb math class. I belong on the beach, where I can soak my feet in caressing water and let the wind wander its way through my chestnut-colored hair and sip Doctor Pepper all day long. I want to grip a straw all day, not a mechanical pencil that will try unsuccessfully to write the answers to unsolvable questions." (Shelly, grade 7)

6. Humor--Professional writers know the value of laughter; even subtle humor can help turn a "boring" paper into one that can raise someone's spirits.

"He laughed? I'm nothing. I'm the rear end of nothing, and the devil himself smiled at me." (Andrew, grade 7)

"And you--yes, you Justin!--were the guilty party who, after I took off my shoes to enjoy the hot pavement in early spring, put a frog in them. Of course, I didn't look at the shoes when I put them back on; it was the **squish** that gave your prank away." (Liz, grade 8)

7. Hyphenated Modifiers--Sometimes a new way of saying something can make all the difference; hyphenated adjectives often cause the reader to "sit up and take notice."

"She's got this blonde hair, with dark highlights, parted in the middle, down past her shoulders, and straight as a preacher. She's got big green eyes that all guys admire and all girls envy, and this **I'm-so-beautiful-and-I-know-it** body, you know, like every other super model." (Ileana, grade 7)

8. Full-Circle Ending--Sometimes students need a special ending, one that effectively "wraps up" the piece. One "trick" is to repeat a phrase from the beginning of the piece.

Beginning:

"Hey, you, with the green and neon-orange striped shoelaces, you who always pulled on my old frazzled white ones in math. Hey, you, who always added your versions of "art" to my math problems for Mrs. Caton's class so that 9 x 7 = 64 turned out to be a train with puffs of smoke and two boxcars and made me get an 83 instead of a 93 since Mrs. C. doesn't count locomotives as correct answers.

Ending:

"Now Justin still sits behind me in math with his neon-green and orange striped shoelaces and pulls on my old white frazzled ones. He still draws zombies on my homework, but he hasn't dumped another pitcher of Kool-Aid on me--not yet at least. Oh, and by the way, in case you're wondering, his first words when he opened his eyes were, "It was James Kenton who hid your clothes and made you walk around in a chicken suit...I'm not that mean." (Liz, grade 8)

Name:__________Class:________________Date:________________

Descriptive Research Requirements

I. Product--Descriptive Research Paper

A. Must be three-five typed pages, double-spaced

B. Must contain at least five researched and documented facts, which could include quoted facts and/or paraphrased facts

1. Internal footnotes will be used as documentation.
2. Internal footnotes will be color-coded according to sources.

C. Must contain documentation from at least three sources

D. Must be centered on a dominant impression supported by three aspects with at least three details per aspect

1. Dominant impression will be labeled.
2. Three aspects will be boxed in.
3. Appropriate transitions will be used.
4. Details will be checked above main words.

E. Must include at least ten smiley-face passages of at least five different types

1. Smiley-face passages will be marked.
2. Smiley-face passages will be labeled by type.

II. Procedure

A. Rough draft will be written in class, using web made from picture.

B. Question note cards will be made regarding information that needs to be looked up in the library.

C. In the library, note cards will be taken, information woven into the story, and documented with the proper internal footnotes and bibliographic information.

D. Rough drafts will be checked by class members in response groups.

E. Student writers will revise their papers according to rubrics.

F. Two final copies will be made for the purpose of presentations, and a picture will be included.

G. Final presentations will involve audience response.

Final due date:______________________

Parent signature:____________________

III. Extra Credit

A. "Props" or extras for presentations
B. Hand-drawn version of picture
C. Other:______________________

Descriptive Research Paper

Teacher Sample

Our Buick Electra 225

It wasn't just the car that was **home** to me then. It was Mama in the car and me riding shotgun, as she would say, like something out of "Paladin" or "Gunsmoke" or "Bonanza" or whatever western was popular during the 50's--I really don't remember. I do remember it wasn't the car just anytime or anyplace; it was the car after school or during summer vacations or on the way to ballet or jazz or tap lessons. The car was home to our CONVERSATIONS, provided us with ENTERTAINMENT, and was a place for us to GROW together.

Sure, I was proud of its sleek lines, its plush seats, and its chrome that Daddy would polish with a vengeance, but it wasn't the car's appearance that I remember so much as Mama's never-ending rush of **conversation** while she drove. Did I realize that Maria Tallchief would be dancing the title role in George Balanchine's The Firebird (WOODRUFF 20) and that Daddy was getting tickets for us to go? And did I know that in my jazz class Mrs. Heidi would be teaching us Martha Graham's famous "falls," where "a dancer contracts, or tightens, her torso and knees as she sinks to the ground, giving in to the force of gravity...then uses the momentum of the fall to rise again" (Garfunkel 25)? At points like this Mama would always gesticulate wildly as if she herself would fall and rise once more right along with old Martha. And could I believe that Rudolf Nureyev, the famous Russian dancer, defected to the United States during a Paris performance (Matheson 613)? Sometimes I would look at Mother as if she were an alien, speaking in a foreign tongue, and I was the stunned Earthling transfixed by her antennae or green, lumpy skin or bulging eyeballs. I didn't know about Maria Tallchief or Martha Graham or Rudolf Nureyev; all I knew was that all of Mama's talking--whatever language she was speaking--soothed me somehow, created a bond. It was Mama, the car, and me.

Besides all the conversation, what took place in the car never failed to **entertain** us both. Mama's black pinhead, as Daddy was wont to say, was barely visible over the giant steering wheel of our white mile-long Buick Electra 225, about which Mama teased Daddy unmercifully. In her opinion, the car magazines had been right when they had proclaimed that the Buicks--at least her Buick, Mama would say with a sly wink--"stopped better than the rest--stopped better than it went, almost" (Nichols 79). Mama had always wanted to be a speed demon, like Barney Olsfield, she always said, but evidently this barge gave her no hope. Anyway, it would have been funny, had it not been so potentially life-threatening, when Mama would turn to face me, as always oblivious to the ever-present eighteen-wheeler eighteen inches in front of her, turn her full attention to me as I sat Indian-style beside her, and suddenly decide to do this thing she did with her braids. At those points it was like the car knew when to steer itself. At precisely the moment Mama would feel her bobby pins slipping, feel her two Pocahontas braids give way and threaten a quick descent from top of her head down her back, the car would sort of lurch forward, throwing itself into auto pilot while Mama would fiddle a good five, ten minutes with both hands on her head. I would stop thinking about tutus or new tap shoes or Mike in math class and start in with the Lord's Prayer. Or maybe Mama would decide to haul out the thermos, pouring us both ice-cold cups of Coca Cola, and I swear she never gave the road a thought. It was as if we were ladies at a tea party sharing a spot on a mid-Victorian sofa, sipping Earl Gray, exchanging pleasantries about the fashions, the weather, lady-like concerns in a lady-like manner.

The real magic of the car, though, EXCLUDING THE CONVERSATION AND THE ENTERTAINMENT, was that Mama and I **grew up** in that car--oh different models, different years, but that never mattered. It was that we watched each other's progress from the front seat of a Buick. See, I was three in that car and I colored in coloring books and played with my Barbies and snuggled next to Mama when I grew tired. And when I turned eleven, I would chew great wads of bubble gum and give the honk-your-horn signal to all passing trucks while I spread my day out before Mama like we were on a hill somewhere perched on a picnic blanket, looking up at the clouds, instead of dodging Houston traffic on the way to dance class. And then at seventeen I would turn up our new state-of-the-art radio full blast and sing along with Elvis's "You Ain't Nothin' but a Hound Dog" and later "Town without Pity" and cried over John Burgin who dumped me for someone older, someone who was allowed to go to Garner State Park without her parents. And Mother was forty-three and then fifty-one and then fifty-seven, and she would tell me that, yes, that was a beautiful picture I had colored and then that I should get my feet off the dashboard, roll up the window, and leave those truckers alone. And--years later--that yes, she understood intellectually why a seventeen-year-old girl would want to drive with her seventeen-year-old friend to Galveston and spend an innocent, sun-loving, spiritually uplifting weekend, but--no--her mind might understand but her heart would never allow it.

"Mama," I would say, changing out of my school clothes and into my tights and leotard, wrapping pink satin toe shoe ribbons around my ankles, "so what's the big deal? Diane and I need a little time off. You know how stressed I've been getting over...over...over algebra, for instance. I mean how many times can a normal human being repeat after Mrs. Platz that the Pythagorean Theorem is "the sum of the squares of the lengths of the legs of a right triangle is equal to the square of the length of the hypotenuse" (JAMES 312) without going bonkers?" I mean I didn't know triangles had legs and what is a hypotenuse anyway? I would smile, thinking that the math ploy would be a good starting point since Mama's monthly math tutoring never failed to lower my "A" average to a "C" when Daddy was out of town giving his "math lectures." Surely Mama would understand Pythagorean trauma--if not the theorem.

"Well, I don't know about that Pithy Theory," Mama would start in.

"Mama, that's Pythagorean," I would try feebly to interject.

"Whatever," Mama might say as she would alternately glance--and I mean glance at the road, like for the first time in five minutes--the rest of her time alternating among trying to figure out if the guy in the truck beside us was watching me as I changed clothes or checking out the progress of the new seafood restaurant on I-45 or trying to pin that stray wisp of hair back so it wouldn't impair her vision of the road that she never really watched anyway. "But I do know my theory. Two young ladies in a resort town like Galveston, a town a whole twenty-seven miles long and three miles wide at its widest point (TYLER 65), a town where, if my memory serves me, Jean Lafitte set up a pirate camp sometime in the early 1800's to get rid of contraband (TYLER 51)--do you hear me contraband, so think of the illegal activities to which two innocent girls could fall victim almost...almost 200 years later--a town where girls wear bikinis right out in the open, a town like that spells trouble with a capital 'T.' Two seventeen-year-old girls in Galveston is simply out of the question. Out of the question. Out--of--the--question."

I always wondered why Mama repeated herself when she was upset. I mean did she think I missed the first "out of the question"? And had I gone into a coma for the second "out of the question"? So the third "out of the question" would be the only one I had heard? Or did she think I was intellectually challenged and had to hear things three times before processing? Or maybe she was of the Mrs. Platz school, the repeat-after-me version of learning. Whatever it was was getting on my nerves and even more now that the answer to my fun-filled vacation was No, No, No.

As I finished dressing, pulling my hair into a ponytail and securing it with a black grosgrain ribbon, Mama finished up with the fact that she had one daughter and no daughter of hers was going anywhere without an army of adults till she was say thirty--okay maybe twenty-five--and that was the end of that, young lady.

But somehow, through it all, we were at home in that car, Mama, and me--just girls on our way to our artistic endeavors, Mama would say, having Mother and Daughter conversations, entertaining each other, and growing together--me spending my youth in that car and Mama her middle age. Nonetheless, we were together, just two girls sometimes even looking at the lay of the land, but always looking to each other--as mothers and daughters--as friends often do.

Works Cited

Garfunkel, Trudy. Letters to the World. Boston: Little, Brown, 1995.

James, Glenn, *et al.* "Pythagorean Theorem." Mathematics Dictionary. 4th ed. 1976.

Matheson, Kay. "Nureyev, Rudolf." World Book Encyclopedia.

Nichols, Richard. Muscle Cars. New York: Exeter Books, 1985.

Tyler, Ron, *ed. et al.* "Galveston Island." The New Handbook of Texas. 6 vols. Austin: Texas State Historical Association, 1996.

---, "Galveston, Texas." The New Handbook of Texas. 6 vols. Austin: Texas State Historical Association, 1996.

Woodruff, Dianne L. "Tallchief, Maria." World Book Encyclopedia.

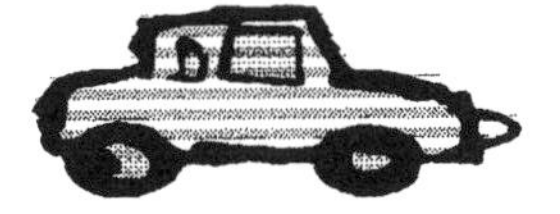

Kelly Ochoa
Descriptive/Narrative Research Paper

Gommy's House

The lake rocks back and forth silently like a mother putting a child to sleep. I wake up to the sweet smell of Swedish pancakes cooking in the oven. I walk downstairs in my robe and onto the porch. Ahhh! Fresh, clean air. I walk back inside to hear Gommy's smiling voice spring up saying, "Your favorite--Swedish pancakes." I sit down as she places a plate in front of me. I don't remember everything we did or where she took me, but I do remember little things like my favorite counter seat or everything being put on hold at 10:00 to flip to "The Price Is Right" on that old turn-the-dial TV that had to be from the mid 1960's with the little screen and the huge box set to hear that reassuring voice: "You're the next contestant on 'The Price Is Right'" **(Cheney 12).** Me and Gommy, Gommy and me, the perfect pair together.

When I would go up every summer for two weeks to the old lakefront house, it was just our time. I started calling Gommy "Gommy" ever since, well, before I can remember. But when I would go up there, I could get away from my parents whose favorite word was always " no," away from my crabby sister, and away from the pressures of life. It was our long conversations, the old mid-Victorian house, and the huge yard I remember most.

It wasn't only the appearance of the house, but the time we spent chatting inside. How should I remember that God made the promise to Abraham and not to David? And the promise was that if Abraham leaves Ur to the country God chooses, God will make him a blessing to all people and make him great **(Batchelor 54).** So I was a little off. Promising David he'll live to see his next birthday while he was in the lion's den was still a better promise. But of course Gommy said, "That's not a promise, is it?" If I have learned one thing about my grandma, it is to never get into a debate about religion.

But we also had other types of conversations. I would tell her about my soccer games and if we won or lost and the never-ending position changes. Then I would explain how soccer is the most popular sport in the world **("Soccer" n.p.).** And she would smile, shaking her head, never saying a word. Not because she was a great listener but because she didn't hear or understand a thing I was saying. But what did get through her ears and mind was frustrating.

"So you say you lost your tennis game?"

"Soccer," I would say.

"Rocker, must be a new sport."

"No, s-o-c-c-e-r!" I would yell.

"Yeah, I know."

She looked at me like I had just given her a multiple-choice question on Newton's first law of motion. Newton's theory is which of the following:

(A) $E=mc^2$

(B) An object in motion tends to stay in motion

(C) Force = mass times acceleration

(D) Weight = mass times gravity

Of course, the answer is "B," but my grandma didn't even "know a guy named Newton" she said. She had this look of confusion on her face, so she would smile and give me that glance of I'm-smiling-just-so-you-will-hush-soon. Not that she was mean; she was the most fun person I have ever met. And even if she didn't understand some things, she always had some bit of advice.

We would sit on the old leather couch while she crocheted quietly. I can still hear, "It really is very easy. It's like knitting a heavy yarn or thread. See, just do a hard-twist cotton thread or try looping single yarn or fabric in a chain **("Crocheting" n.p.).** I looked at the thread, spellbound. While I would try desperately to get the crochet needle out of the knot I had made, she would talk about her life as a kid and how she couldn't have lived without her grandmother. But there were funny times, too, like when she told me about my dad and grandpa trying to fix the lights. Once they were done, every time someone rang the doorbell, the lights would come on and every time someone turned on the lights, the doorbell would ring. It was just me and Gommy, having one of our great days by doing absolutely nothing.

BESIDES OUR CONVERSATIONS, I loved the house, the huge building with the saltillo floors and the big wooden porch. It had an old-timey, mid-Victorian look, with a giant staircase I could slide down, an old rug with a bean-bag chair where I could watch TV, and steps to the kitchen I could easily trip on. I remember my sister and me putting on a fashion show in the garage. We dressed up in Gommy's rain gear and came into the den like waddling ducks trying to fill colossal shoes, which were only a size seven. As we waddled around aimlessly, I can still hear my mom, "That's my daughters all right." She was right.

Besides our fashion shows, the first thing I would think about the house is that it was like a museum. When I was little, I didn't understand why I couldn't bounce a ball in the house, which I still don't understand now either. And I would listen to my mom, the wild ape, preach on at the pulpit about the great-great this, the original these, and the great-great that. Of course, to be an antique it would have had to have been bought by my great-great grandma when it was new. We've all heard the sermon that to be an antique, furniture must be at least 100 years old, but between new and 100 years old, furniture is just considered old **("Antiques" n.p.).** And no, I couldn't bounce the ball in the house and, no, I couldn't eat in the den and, no, I couldn't see if the neighbors' electric fence worked.

Oh, but then there was the game room--my room. There were coloring books with a huge bucket of crayons, a small TV, a big don't-touch desk, and the trunk. Yes, the trunk. I'd listen to the TV while I plowed through the trunk until I found my favorite dolls and played with them in their three-story house. Some days it was an airplane house, others a boat house. My favorite, though, was the Malibu beach house. Then I would hear those fateful words on the news, "The time is now 9 p.m." and I would hear Gommy's happy voice, "Time for bed." I forced the news anchor to take it back. But no, he didn't; he just smiled. So, yes, I did have to go to bed, trouping slowly to my room. But I'd try to go to bed quickly so I could wake up again and it would be the morning.

ALTHOUGH I LOVED TALKING AND THE HOUSE HELD MANY SECRETS, **the yard was a wonder.** About two or three summers ago, I went up there and took tennis lessons. Gommy told me she'd pick me up, but she wasn't there, so I decided to walk home. Her neighborhood is a huge maze. Naturally, I got lost. I was wandering around when a man pulled over and said, "Lost? Hop in."

I wasn't thinking so I shut the door, and the thought entered my mind, "Stupid, he could be a kidnapper or a murderer." But I stayed cool and luckily I knew the street name, and when we found my grandma's street I recognized it. It wasn't the house, but the yard with the big pine trees and the winding sidewalk that were just the clues I had been waiting for. The yard. My oasis. Not only for me but for the deer. Yes, the deer as well, who would come every morning. Gommy and I would feed the squirrels corn, the geese and ducks feed, the catfish bread and deer alfalfa. We supported all the wildlife in Elkin's Lake. And if we were lucky, every day around 9:00 a.m. and 9:00 p.m. about fourteen deer would come eat. Gommy and I would wake up at 8:00, get ready, and go outside to sit on the bench. We left the feed out, and slowly and cautiously the deer approached. We had to be perfectly still; any sudden movements and the deer would bolt like rabbits, flashing their white tails of danger, warning the other deer **(Hinshaw 18).** Besides the deer, there was the lake. We had our own little dock with two love seats, where my sister and I would fish for hours. She would bait her hook and wait and get nothing. I didn't understand the concept of bait so I didn't use any and caught my first fish in its eye. I ran inside for a Band-Aid, but my mom wouldn't let me stick his eye back on. Beside the dock was the paddle boat, bug-yellow and very heavy. My sister and I would go out on the lake for hours. We called a small dry spot Snake Island, and my sister would scare me with vivid descriptions of extraterrestrial snakes. Even though there were an alligator and snakes in the lake, I still loved that lake with all my heart.

The lake rocks back and forth still, but my grandma and I aren't there to see it. Gommy and I still have conversations, but not in the same house. The colossal house still stands, but we don't visit it. No, my grandma has moved, and times have changed. I like her living in my neighborhood now, but I'll never forget the other house. These days we spend time in the new house with the old antiques, and I play in the new yard. But I'll never forget Gommy's and my special times at the old place. Just the two of us, the perfect pair, just Gommy and me having wonderful days doing absolutely nothing.

Peri Arthur
Descriptive Research Paper

The Garden

The garden, our garden, what a mystical place. It always made us feel like we were in some faraway setting or in the movie The Secret Garden. It was Ginger and I, just the two of us there in the garden, but it really wasn't just the two of us. There were the roses, the jasmine, and the ivy, too. The wind chimes would chime a song for us as we would dance in the wind. Even the fish in the pond would be particularly happy on those afternoons. The flowers would seem softer, the breeze sweeter, and the waterfall more tranquil on the days Ginger and I played our imaginary music. Ginger is, yes, a dog, but that made it even more magical because when the flowers would go back to their places, the wind would calm, and I eventually grew up, we both realized that there was no one who would tell our childhood secrets. I can't remember the first day I truly appreciated the garden, noticed its rare beauty, and actually began to love it. All I know is that the garden was my sanctuary, a place of **refuge**, a **place to let my imagination run wild** like I was still three, a **place that gave me confidence** to go out and face the world.

It wasn't just the garden that I loved, but the fact that **it was my refuge away from the world.** Outside the garden was the basketball hoop I would play on in the summer. It seemed as if the garden helped me play. Of course, back then I didn't know what I later learned--that James Naismith invented basketball at the YMCA in December of 1891 **("Basketball" n.p.).** I was just there because the guys were there. After our games we would go back to the garden, every one of us, and my mom would have smoked cocktail weenies ready and waiting. We would sit and eat like that was what we did everyday. But then there were those days when I would try to play football with my brother on the St. Augustine grass. I envisioned myself to be like Troy Aikman when he led the Dallas Cowboys to two consecutive super bowls **("Aikman, Troy" n.p.),** that is until I got hit in the head and refused to ever play again. At that point I ran to the one and only bench we had on our patio, my only shelter from humiliation, and vowed to be a cheerleader from there on. Of course, there was the time when I was practicing my volleyball serves and hit the ball right through the garage window. It was so funny that I ran into the garden and laughed so hard I thought my stomach would pop like a balloon. I loved those days when I tried to be one of the guys, and the garden knew it.

NOT ONLY WAS MY GARDEN A REFUGE, but **it was a place for my imagination to**

run wild. I remember going into the garden and loving the sun pouring down rays of light on our natural umbrella of tree limbs. The sun felt rich and full in those days. The jasmine was as sweet as Starbursts on a hot day, melting in our mouths, the water in the pond as cool as a spring rain, and the flowers gave me an I-want-to-be-touched look. Everything was perfect for my little garden cottage. I made spoons out of shells and sticks and picked herbs of clover, rosemary, mint, oregano, and thyme, not knowing that I could have cleverly used them as perfume as the Asians do **("Thyme" n.p.).** The wild strawberries squished in my mouth with a gush of juice down my chin. I played on the swing, being a pirate on an ocean shore, or I was a gypsy, fighting dragons and monsters, or I was a princess dancing on a ballroom floor. My garden allowed me to be anything.

All of my dreams and fantasies and imaginary happenings were just as real as the drip drop, plip plop of rain that often fell on my face, snapping me back to reality. I couldn't understand why God would make it rain. Just as well, I figured, as I would jump off the swing and land with a splat on the flat pieces of limestone--not caring about what Daddy had said, something about that they contained magnesium something or other and quartz and that his construction company used my rocks as building stones **("Rock" n.p.).** I would gather myself up and run into the house to wait on the rain to stop so

I could dream my dreams in the garden once more.

THE GARDEN WASN'T JUST A PLACE FOR ME TO RUN TO WHEN I WANTED TO BE ALONE OR TO DREAM, but it was a mother, father, sister or brother, something that always seemed to listen. The only difference was that I didn't have to tell it the reason for feeling the way I did. It just kind of knew. When one of those dreaded days, or even one of the best days happened, I could run to the garden, and it would forever give me confidence. When my grandmother, Nana, passed away, I ran to the garden with such a vengeance that I could have killed God. Of course, I wouldn't have, but I wanted to strike out at anyone who could take Nana from me. I loved her and she was the first actual person that I was close to who had died. When I reached the garden that day, all I could do was think and cry. It gave me a new understanding. I didn't understand why she had to die, but the garden made me realize that she would miss me just as much as I would miss her. The garden was my listener, the person for whom I longed, the one I couldn't wait to see. I remember the time my best guy friend came over. I've never told anyone, except the garden, that he was my crush too. I was surprised that he came over to my house, but it seemed natural to take him to my favorite place. Out in the garden we talked on the swing for hours, it seemed, and once he left I went right back to the garden and relived every moment. I felt as happy as Shannon Miller when she won five Olympic gymnastic medals, the most ever won by an American, in the 1992 Olympic games **("Miller, Shannon" n.p.),** and I could almost hear the garden saying, "He really likes you." I couldn't have been happier. The garden seemed to really help me the most, though, when I didn't get into the finals at UIL. Everyone was behind me--my coach, my parents, my friends, my teachers. I was competing in the Oral Reading, my poem was great, and I had it down to a science. When I read it to classes as practice, some of the teachers cried, and some kids came up to me in the hall to tell me how well I had done. But when I didn't place and kids would ask what I had won, all I could reply was "Nothing, but I'll try harder next time." The only thing I could do was to run to my garden and scream. Not just a scream, but an I-could-die scream. It hurt so much, but somehow after sitting in the garden I didn't feel perfectly happy, but I was content, and I told myself there was always room for improvement.

The garden was everything I could ever want in a best friend. Some people may think I'm crazy to love a place so much, but the garden is a place for me to run to, play in, and just think things through. For some kids my garden would be like a tree house, but I have something better, for mine is made of love, not wood.

Jared Wilson
Descriptive Research Paper

Garner State Park

Garner, it was a word that all our family had grown to love, a place where we knew that once a year we would end up. Garner, our favorite vacation spot, was named after John Nance Garner **(Tyler 97)**, the vice-president of the United States who served from 1933-1941 **("Garner, John" n.p.).** Each summer when the day came, we were ready, and when our parents came in and woke us, we were up, ready, and in the car before any of us kids really realized it. The whole trip wasn't just being there. It was getting there too, but it was also the **ride in the car,** the **fun we all had**, and the **let's-all-go-cram-into-one-tent-and-see-if-we-can-fall-asleep-before-morning-comes nights.**

Sure, we liked being there, but **it was a challenge getting there**. On the way, the car became our best friend. We found totally useless information that we never knew. Who would have guessed that there are thirty-four stripes on our back seat or that there are eight cup holders, but that we only use five of them or that Dad would lock the windows after rolling and unrolling them at least twenty times. When kids are just sitting in a car for six hours--at least the kids in our family--we would do anything to pass the time. We'd play those I'm-bored-give-me-something-to-do games like road sign A,B,C's or car Bingo or those electronic hand-held games that we never found fun until we took them on a road trip. We also found out things that we had once thought were impossible were indeed in the realm of reality, like four of us fitting into a space two-feet wide and three-feet long and actually being able to fall asleep in it. Maybe it was then that we understood the phenomenon that the ride to a destination always seems longer than the ride back--we were used to it! Yes, it was the car that seemed like our best friend for six hours of every year.

BESIDES THE RIDE OVER THERE, **the rest of the trip was fun.** We all loved being there and never once were bored. It was a tradition that all of our parents and older brothers played volleyball while we younger kids sat on the sidelines and watched, hoping that someone would have to leave so that we could have a slim chance to be considered as a candidate to take his spot. Sometimes they would just play without a player so they wouldn't be stuck with one of us. "But we're good," we'd plead. "If I'm on your team, we'll surely win," or at least that is what we thought and told them with regularity. But when they all had to leave (or all got tired of playing), we finally got the court, but we usually couldn't play because we had six players, four of whom were little kids that couldn't hit the ball if--as the cliche goes--their lives depended on it. If we weren't playing volleyball, we were shooting water balloons at the people floating down the 200-mile-long river **(Tyler 97)** or watching the forty-four different species of animals at Garner **(Tyler 97).** If we were lucky, we would knock someone out of his tube, and if we were really lucky, he would get out of the water and start running at us with one of those you're-going-to-wish-you-never-did-that looks. But each year, when the unlucky fellow would get to the cliff and find he didn't have a way up, he would just say a few choice words, we would continue to taunt him with water balloons, and he would finally leave, defeated.

THOUGH THE RIDE UP THERE AND THE FUN WE ALL SHARED WERE A MAJOR PART OF THE TRIP, **the most fun part was the nights.** We usually started the nights off running around in almost endless circles, chasing fireflies giving out bright mating signals **("Firefly" n.p.),** trying to catch them so the little kids could put them in a jar and watch their antics. Or we would stare up at the black night sky until we all had headaches, trying to see who could spot the most satellites, sometimes getting so dizzy that we could have sworn we had seen one where nothing of the kind existed. Then we all would cram into one tent and see if we could fall asleep. In the morning we would wake up and invariably run into a tree that we swore had not been there the previous day. Or maybe we would listen to the stories the others would tell: "Where did you get that black eye?" someone would ask. "You hit me, you idiot," would be the reply.

But through it all, **the best thing that would happen would be that we all would have grown closer as friends.** I guess it was the ride there or the fun we all had together or those let's-all-go-cram-into-one-tent-and-see-if-we-can-fall-asleep-before-morning-comes nights. When we look back--and each and every year we always do--we realize that all in all it was another good vacation at Garner.

Name:______________________________Class:______________Date:____________________

Descriptive Research Rubric #1

To prove that you have done the following research skills correctly, quote appropriate passages from your descriptive research paper. If you realize from the examples that you have made mistakes on your rough draft, revise your paper and then quote the correct version below.

1. In your own words write a question you researched (one that I have not checked in the library) and the answer:

   a. Question:____

   ____

   b. Answer:____

   ____

2. To illustrate that you have blended the researched information with your own words, quote a passage from your paper, including the research and internal documentation.

☞ Remember the following points:

a. If you are using a quotation (as opposed to paraphrased information), you must blend the quoted material with your words; a quotation can never stand alone.

b. An internal footnote is the author's last name--or the article title placed in quotation marks if there is no author--and page number.

c. There is no mark of punctuation between the author's name and the page: (Woodall 23) or ("Hawaii" n.p.).

d. You must document all researched information even if that information is paraphrased.

e. Place a period after the footnote unless the footnote comes in the middle of the sentence.

Quote your sentence here:

____

____

____

____

3. Plagiarism occurs when you use three or four of an author's words in succession without quoting. Give an example of researched information that you have paraphrased (other than the example in #2) and the footnote.

____

____

____

Name:__________________Class:__________________Date:__________

Descriptive Research Rubric #2

To ensure that you have followed the requirements of the descriptive research paper, quote the following from your work. If you need to revise your paper, do so; then quote the correct version below.

I. Smiley-Face Passages—List your five best smiley-face passages and state the type of each by using your "Smiley-Face Tricks" sheet.

☺ Be sure you have at least ten labeled in your paper.

a. ____

____

____

____

Type: ____________________

b. ____

____

____

Type: ____________________

c. ____
____
____

Type: ________________

d. ____
____
____

Type: ________________

e. ______________________________
____
____
____

Type: ________________

II. Structure--Using your web, outline your paper. Remember that each Roman numeral must be parallel (the same part of speech) as all other Roman numerals and that all subdivisions must be parallel with each other.

☺Outline your paper using the following guide:

I. Introduction--Thesis: ________________________
____
____

☺ Remember that your **three aspects** must be stated in your thesis, they must be **parallel with each other grammatically**, and they must be listed in the **order that they are covered** in your paper.

II. First Main Point:______________________________

A. Details________________
B. ______________________
C. ______________________

III. Second Main Point:______________________________

A. Details________________
B. ______________________
C. ______________________

IV. Third Main Point:______________________________

A. Details________________
B. ______________________
C. ______________________

V. Conclusion--Restatement of Thesis:____

III. Transitions--Quote the **three main transitions** that begin each body paragraph:

A. First Body:______________________________
B. Second Body

☺Remember to include the MAIN point from your first body:______________________

____

C. Third Body

☺Remember to include the points from your first two bodies:______________________

____

iv. IMAGERY--IF YOU HAVE USED ENOUGH IMAGERY OR WORD PICTURES IN YOUR DESCRIPTIVE PAPER, YOUR READER SHOULD BE ABLE TO ENVISION THE PLACE YOU ARE DESCRIBING. DRAW AND LABEL THE PICTURE THAT YOU WANT YOUR READERS TO ENVISION.

NAME:________________ CLASS:________________ DATE:__________

Descriptive Research Paper Final Check Sheet

YOUR **RESEARCH PACKET** SHOULD CONTAIN THE COMPONENTS LISTED BELOW AND BE IN THE **FOLLOWING ORDER**. PUT A CHECK MARK BY EACH REQUIREMENT WHEN YOU HAVE COMPLETED IT.

I. _____COVER SHEET
- _____A. TITLE IN CENTER
- _____B. HEADING IN LOWER RIGHT-HAND CORNER

II. _____PICTURE--ORIGINAL PICTURE THAT INSPIRED THE WRITING (MAY BE PHOTOGRAPH, MAGAZINE CLIPPING, OR HAND-DRAWN SKETCH)

III. _____OUTLINE
- _____A. MUST CONTAIN FIVE ROMAN NUMERALS
- _____B. ROMAN NUMERALS II-IV MUST HAVE AT LEAST THREE SUBDIVISIONS
- _____C. FIRST LETTERS OF EACH ENTRY MUST BE CAPITALIZED
- _____D. ALL ENTRIES MUST BE IN PARALLEL STRUCTURE (SAME PART OF SPEECH)

IV._______FINAL COPIES (TWO FINAL COPIES: ONE FOR YOU TO READ TO CLASS; THE OTHER FOR THE TEACHER TO MARK MISTAKES, QUESTIONS FOR THE CLASS, ETC. AS YOU READ)
- _______ A. THESIS IN BRACKETS
- _______ B. THREE ASPECTS CHECKED IN THESIS
- _______ C. TRANSITION WORDS/PHRASES FOR EACH BODY PARAGRAPH CIRCLED
- _______ D. MAJOR POINTS BOXED IN

DESCRIPTIVE RESEARCH PAPER FINAL CHECK SHEET

_______ E. DETAILS IN EACH BODY CHECK-MARKED
_______ F. FOOTNOTES COLOR-CODED ACCORDING TO AUTHOR
_______ G. TEN SMILEY-FACE PASSAGES MARKED AND LABELED BY TYPE (SEE "SMILEY-FACE TRICKS" SHEET)
_______ H. PARENT SIGNATURE (ON FINAL DRAFT)

V.______NOTE CARDS
_______ A. COLOR-CODED ACCORDING TO AUTHOR
_______ B. STAPLED TO BLANK SHEET(S) OF PAPER

VI.____ BIBLIOGRAPHY
_______A. ENTRIES MUST BE ALPHABETIZED
_______B. ENTRIES MUST NOT BE NUMBERED
_______C. ENTRIES MUST BE PUNCTUATED ACCORDING TO MLA FORMAT

VII.____ RUBRICS--CORRECTIONS ON RUBRICS MUST BE USED TO REVISE PAPER.
_______A. RUBRIC #1 MUST BE INCLUDED
_______B. RUBRIC #2 MUST BE INCLUDED

VIII.___ROUGH DRAFT(S)

IX._____CIRCLE RESPONSE SHEET

X._______REQUIREMENT SHEET (SIGNED BY PARENTS)

XI._____EXTRA CREDIT

A+

PART VI

HOW-TO (PROCESS) RESEARCH

Using You Are the Teacher

1. Students should be given opportunities to write from the **point of view** of someone other than themselves. **"You Are the Teacher"** asks students to imagine what a teacher might do to follow *CURRICULUM GUIDELINES*.

2. Besides writing from a different perspective, **"You Are the Teacher"** reinforces the **how-to mode** in that it requires students to write **three clearly defined steps** in teaching a particular novel/library book.

3. The assignment also asks that students **use quoted material from the text,** which gives them practice *BLENDING QUOTATIONS, USING INTERNAL FOOTNOTES, AND SUPPORTING THEIR OWN THINKING WITH EXCERPTS FROM A LITERARY WORK.*

4. Papers can be **read in class** or in small groups to **acquaint classmates with books** that they might like to read.

Library Book Test
How-To Mode

Name:________________________ Class:____________________ Date:______________

You Are the Teacher!

Assignment:

1. The curriculum for your school mandates that the book entitled____________________________________ **be taught** to your class. You, as the teacher, want the students to be interested in the book; therefore, motivational strategies will play an important role as will the literary concepts to be covered.

2. Your coordinator would like you to submit a five-paragraph plan that outlines how you intend to approach this piece. She wants to make sure that textual material is being used as support and has required that each of your three main points be exemplified by quotations from the book.

3. Your first step is to web your three areas, the three steps you will use to enable your students to enjoy the book as well as learn from it. Remember that each step must have two substeps, two details for support. Your substeps could be the quoted material you wish to incorporate.

4. Your next step is to write your rough draft; your final step is the final draft.

Rubric:

1. Remember that you must get the **idea of the book** across. Your coordinator will want to be sure that you have read the book in its entirety.

2. All quoted material must be introduced with your own words. Remember that the point should be made in your words with the author's as support for your own thinking.

3. The format of the five-paragraph plan is a how-to, which necessitates your giving your coordinator three clear steps as an outline for teaching the book.

4. Of course, your mechanics (RUN-ONS, FRAGMENTS, ETC.) as well as your spelling will count in that they help convey an overall impression of your work.

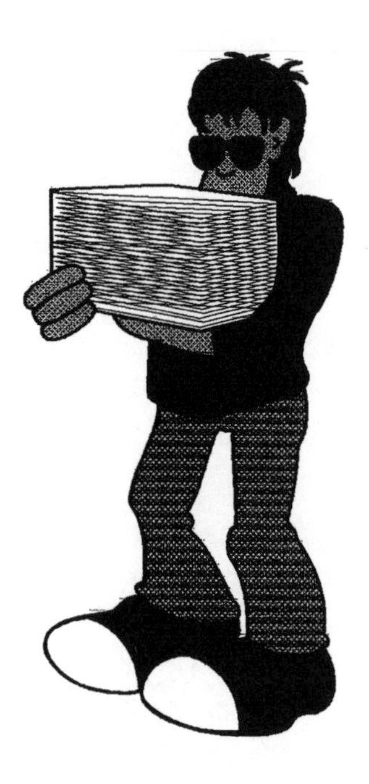

Jacques Pouhe
You Are the Teacher!

To: Dr. Payne
From: Professor Jacques Pouche
Date: January 21
Re: Library Book/Curriculum

I have recently read the novel <u>Where'd You Get the Gun, Billy?</u> and decided that it is the perfect story to teach my literature class. The narrative explores the terrible potential of violence in the quaint, quiet town of Crestview and sheds light on the deadly consequences of possession of dangerous weapons. This book will teach my students to recognize how literature can relate to their lives. That magical relationship between the book and the student is one of the many things that they will learn to enjoy. From this book they will also learn how to make intelligent inferences and how to identify and categorize conflicts.

The first lesson I would teach my students is how to make **inferences** based on information in the text. To begin, I'd define inference as a conclusion or decision derived from something known or assumed. Then, I'd give students examples of real-life inferences, such as if a man dresses in expensive clothes and drives a new sedan, we can infer that he is rich or that he likes to spend his money on smooth clothes and flashy cars. Next, I'd ask students to make an inference about the book by the title alone. The answer I'd expect to get is something to the effect that the book must have some violence in it, and because the title itself poses a question, that it might be a mystery. Finally, I'd read to them the excerpt: "**Ellen's face was tear-stained**" (13) and ask for an inference. I'd anticipate a response that they can infer that Ellen and Lisa are close because Ellen can't stop crying over Lisa's death.

Besides the lesson on inference, I would teach students how to recognize the ways **certain aspects of the book can relate to them,** to their own lives. They would do this by first choosing an aspect of the book and examining it from every angle possible. Suppose they choose to examine the principal, Mr. Elwood, and they read the part where he says, " 'I mean…I really can't believe something like this could…I mean big cities with drugs and crime, yeah, but Crestview [referring to the shooting in the school]?' " Students might discover that they feel like Mr. Elwood in that they never would expect something big to happen in their small town either. Suppose they choose to look at Liz, Lisa's "closest friend" (6), the girl who is shot by her boyfriend. Because of the loss of her friend, she feels "all broken up inside" (7) so she "did her crying" (6) all too often. Many might then realize that they relate to Liz because they, once too, might have lost a close friend and mourned over the loss.

Not only would students learn inference and personal identification, they would be given the opportunity to recognize conflicts and identify whether they are external or internal. To do this, I would first define both conflicts with everyday examples. Then I would choose conflicts from the novel for students to categorize. They would first be assigned the quotation: " 'Hey, listen, I didn't mean it!' Billy cried. They were pushing his head down now, forcing him into the backseat of the sedan. 'I loved her, David! I swear I didn't mean it' " (27). Students would conclude that since Billy is apologizing for his actions and feeling at fault with his own wrong-doings, he is having an internal conflict; however, the force being used represents external conflict. Then, I would ask them to analyze the quote: "She never thought she could hate Charlie, but right at that moment what she was feeling seemed terribly close to hate" (45). Students would see the complexity in this situation in that it is internal, involving her feelings, yet it could appear to be external as well since it involves anger directed at another, therefore man vs. man.

I believe that <u>Where'd You Get the Gun, Billy?</u> and my lessons will teach students many skills: making intelligent inferences, recognizing relationships between the book and their own situations, and categorizing conflicts.

NAME: ______________________ CLASS: ____________ DATE: __________

Research Paper How-To Mode

Product:

1. How-to research paper containing the following:
   - A. **Introduction**--thesis and three points
   - B. **Three aspects**
     1. A minimum of two points per aspect
     2. A minimum of two footnotes per aspect
   - C. **Conclusion**--restatement of thesis and three points

   Each part must be typed on a separate page. Make two final drafts for presentation purposes.

2. Web and Outline

3. **Works Cited**--minimum of five sources, at least three different types

4. **Topics**--You will choose from the attached list; no two students will do the same topic. You must sign up with me and have your choice approved.

5. Note cards
   - A. **Vocabulary note cards**--Ten specialized vocabulary note cards, quoting passages from reading, giving internal footnotes, and defining terms.
   - B. **Topic note cards**--A minimum of thirty other note cards
   - C. **Bibliographic cards**--a minimum of five separate sources

NAME: ______________________ **CLASS:** ____________ **DATE:** __________

Research Topics for How-To Essay

1. How to cope with family violence
2. How to cope with harassment
3. How to work toward agreement
4. How to be popular
5. How to make decisions
6. How to invest in the stock market
7. How to live with a single parent
8. How to cope with cliques
9. How to baby-sit
10. How to overcome prejudice
11. How to show respect
12. How to make a difference in our society
13. How to get along with teachers
14. How to make money
15. How to stand up for your rights
16. How to be healthy
17. How to truly trust people
18. How to overcome your fears
19. How to overcome depression
20. How to be happy
21. How to save energy
22. How to help the environment
23. How to express yourself
24. How to plan an overseas trip
25. How to be a body builder
26. How to diet successfully
27. How to care for your body
28. How to cope with body changes
29. How to get along with siblings
30. How to cope with addiction
31. How to write poetry
32. How to cook healthy foods
33. How to decorate
34. How to win contests
35. How to get published

RESEARCH TOPICS FOR HOW-TO ESSAY

36. How to build a better vocabulary
37. How to learn sign language
38. How to be successful in science
39. How to have an award-winning science experiment
40. How to have proper etiquette
41. How to throw a successful party
42. How to develop your singing voice
43. How to play an instrument
44. How to be a juggler
45. How to be a magician
46. How to be funny
47. How to debate
48. How to draw
49. How to give a speech
50. How to plant a garden
51. How to improve your grammar
52. How to improve your reading comprehension
53. How to sharpen your study skills
54. How to collect stamps
55. How to cope with death
56. How to improve your S.A.T. scores
57. How to improve your scores on math tests
58. How to improve your scores in science
59. How to improve your scores in reading
60. How to improve your scores in writing
61. How to measure the volume of a rock
62. How to get electricity from a food source
63. How to make a dichotomous key
64. How to classify plants/animals
65. How to identify land forms
66. How to be an impresario
67. How to be an explorer
68. How to start a revolution
69. How to strengthen your geography skills
70. How to lose a battle
71. How to start your own business
72. How to establish peace between countries
73. How to discriminate
74. How to be the perfect housewife of the '50's
75. How to locate the constellations
76. How to distinguish among acids, bases, and salts
77. How to play chess
78. How to locate, distinguish among, and plant wild flowers
79. How to show F.F.A. animals

80. How to position, time, and acceleration
81. How to forecast the weather
82. How to appreciate art
83. How to be a ruler (emperor, king, president, queen)
84. How to conquer a country
85. How to cross _________ (the Alps, the Rockies, the English Channel)
86. How to invent _________ (cotton gin, etc.)
87. How to be a good math (science, etc.) teacher
88. How to dance
89. How to play a sport
90. How to be a heart

TEACHER MODEL
Research Paper
How-To Mode

The Business of Writing

(INTRODUCTION)

Who hasn't been invited to speak at a formal function--as president of the class, as president of the board, or to presidents--and while the speaking doesn't pose a problem, the writing of the speech does. Or maybe we've always wanted to write a short story, a really good short story, one that will be read and reread for years to come. Or maybe we simply want to get an "A" on an English assignment, finally to prove to the Mrs. Peabodys of the world that we have what it takes. But we sit at our desks, stare at our blank papers, and wonder just what the tricks of writing really are. [If we follow three simple steps--√believe in the power of our subconscious, √shape our writing, and √revise--we'll be on the road to successful writing in no time.]

(FIRST ASPECT)

So how come this business of writing seems so effortless for some people? What's the first key to success? Perhaps in writing, as in life, the trick is to believe in ourselves, to believe that we can make it happen, have faith in our subconscious. Ray Bradbury believes that every day with just a word or two to trigger his imagination he can unlock his subconscious and let all sorts of images take him where they want him to go, the "treats and tricks...[of] word association" (Bradbury 15), as he calls it. For instance, the word "carnival" evoked childhood memories that Bradbury had half-forgotten, but before long the word turned into the story (Bradbury 18), which turned into the play, which was made into a movie--Something Wicked This Way Comes. All the complexities of characterization, a mysterious, exciting plot, the theme of good versus evil--all emerged from a single word buried deep inside the writer until that morning his typewriter--seemingly out of nowhere--formed the letters. Bradbury believed in his imagination, and it didn't--it hasn't--let him down. He says that "there's no difference between a short story and life" (Strickland

54), and if we've read his 300 short stories, his 25 books of fiction, poems, plays, and essays (Strickland 55), we can only agree. But if our ideas don't "dance out of...[our] subconscious" (Strickland 54), perhaps we need more of a jumpstart than Bradbury does.

Gabriele Rico attests to the power of clustering. Rico's convincing analogy has its basis in nature. She tells writers to "think of the nearly infinite number of seeds that fall to earth, only a fraction of which take root to become trees" (Rico 28). Rico's theory is that the same holds true for writing when writers "explore an astronomical number of possible patterns before settling on an idea" (28). If the word itself--carnival--won't get the juices going, Ricco would say to associate, to ask ourselves what that childhood carnival looked like, to describe the sights, sounds, smells, tastes, feelings as they come to us, and out of this clustering of memories the best will remain, like wheat separated from its chaff.

Then there are the writers and teachers of writing like Dan Kirby and Tom Liner who realize that some writers need whole vignettes out of which ideas can be formed. These writers use journals to "write more frequently and for longer periods of time" (Kirby and Liner 46); these journal writings then become an "idea market, a place where students explore ideas that interest them alone" (46). Whatever the method we choose, the point is to get in touch with our subconscious, to create an atmosphere of freedom, to be receptive to the pouring out of ideas that will follow.

(SECOND ASPECT)

So our thoughts are flowing, we've found our muse, writer's block is no longer a worry, how do we shape our ideas into a coherent, meaningful form? Let's face it--we can freewrite till the proverbial cows come home and have a product that is expressive and could be classified under "Remembrances" or "Recollections" or some other personal category, but how do we write for a wider audience? It's simple if we "never lose sight of the person on the other side of the page" (Cheney). That's where the acronym **SOAP** (Subject, Occasion, Audience, and Purpose) comes into play. If our **SUBJECT** is the two-headed, purple people-eater discovered in downtown Detroit, we've got to stick with it. We can't switch to all our sister's faults--however tempted we are and however much she reminds us of our original topic. And if our **OCCASION** is an important assignment and our **AUDIENCE** is our teacher, we should humor him or her and throw in some standard, formal English--all the rules we've been taught for eons. If our **PURPOSE** is to compare and contrast, for instance, we can do it in a number of ways, but we must make sure we have clear similarities and differences.

What could be easier? Writing is like anything else--we do what's appropriate. We wouldn't wear tennis shoes and overalls to our formal presentation; similarly we wouldn't write our speech to the president of the board in informal language. If we want to convince someone to believe in something we feel strongly about, we wouldn't simply tell a story unless that story were an example of one of our clearly defined reasons. Now if we want to entertain, if we want to weave a tale that someone will read late at night, then a narrative is for us. English teachers have worn their voices and their students out for centuries making the simple more complex than it really is. All we need to keep in mind is what Robert Frost writes in his "Short Talk on Poetry": "The beautiful is the appropriate, that which serves....A five-gallon hat on a cowboy riding a horse on an Arizona ranch is beautiful--but the same hat on a crowded city streetcar would be out of place, inappropriate" (Frost 413). It's the same with writing.

(THIRD ASPECT)

The ideas have now flowed freely, have taken shape, have worked toward a set purpose, now what? Now it's time to do what we're supposed to do in all aspects of real life--give it our best shot; revise. When our beloved, brand-new puppy does the unmentionable on our beloved, brand-new carpet, we work on the stain, work on it again, and work on it some more until we get it out--until we're satisfied. If we're athletes, we practice that jump shot or jackknife dive or that pass to the end zone until we can do them in our sleep. Well, it's the same with writing. Writers and teachers of writing call it revision, which means "reseeing." If we think of our writing like the quest for that perfect gift to give to that special person, then--like our undaunted search for that magical item, that one gift that will prove our love--our poem or short story or essay will be right only when it's the very best we can do. In essence, our writing is like a gift--it comes from the heart, it represents us, and it's the perfect tangible "message" for that person. Columnist Ellen Goodman says, "What makes me happy is rewriting....It's like cleaning house, getting rid of all the junk, getting things in the right order, tightening up" (qtd. in Nadell 89). In this stage of the process, we get out our brooms and our dust pans and go to work. One thing we might need to rework is our sentence structure. Have we eliminated redundancy, replaced weak phrases with strong ones, varied our sentence structure type and length? (Nadell 102-112) Peter Elbow states that one major benefit of revising our sentence structure is that often "new and better ideas arrive. They don't come out of the blue. They come from noticing difficulties with...small details" (Elbow 131). Sometimes, then, what begins as a simple sentence revision might lead us to deeper structural changes which will produce a whole new product. We set out to replace a weak phrase and we sometimes are rewarded with an entirely new, stronger paragraph. Our last stage of revision is the grammatical "clean up." Since "grammar is writing's surface," (Elbow 168) it's often what people notice first about our paper--our presentation. How do we check for spelling, punctuation, subject/verb agreement, and pronoun usage--virtually all those types of errors we've been lectured on since we first set foot in school? Elbow suggests that we "sneak up on grammar" by choosing a few mistakes each time we catch them in our editing process and recording them in a notebook (Elbow 171). He also offers tips such as reading from a typed draft, taking a break, and reading aloud (Elbow 170). So we must remember not to be easily satisfied, not to accept shoddy material. We'd send back a meal that was not prepared to our specifications, we'd ask painters to touch up areas they missed, so we must send our writing back for a second try and touch up areas we overlooked the first time.

(CONCLUSION)

Now the president's impressed and has agreed with our well presented ideas, or we've written that story that has kept whole classes spellbound, or research papers have come back marked "A! Loved your ideas! Thanks for providing a new slant on the subject!" [At last our writing is going somewhere, thanks to √believing in the power of our subconscious, √shaping our writing, and √revising.] Now we finally understand the business of writing.

Works Cited

Bradbury, Ray. Zen in the Art of Writing. New York: Bantam, 1990.

Cheney, Theodore A. Rees. Getting the Words Right. Cincinnati: Writer's Digest Books, 1983.

Elbow, Peter. Writing With Power. New York: Oxford, 1981.

Frost, Robert. "Short Talk on Poetry." Introduction to Literature. Ed. Edward J. Gordon. Lexington, MA: Ginn, 1978. 411-418.

Kirby, Dan and Tom Liner. Inside Out. New York: Boynton/Cook, 1981.

Nadell, Judith, Linda McMeniman, and John Langan. The Macmillan Writer. New York: Macmillan, 1994.

Rico, Gabriele Lusser. Writing the Natural Way. Los Angeles: J. P. Tarcher, 1983.

Strickland, Bill, ed. On Being a Writer. Cincinnati: Writer's Digest Books, 1989.

Nikki Thompson
How-To Research Paper

How to Be a Heart

Introduction

Herman Heart busily pumps blood through our bodies and makes small talk with our veins. His life is very interesting, but the blood cells think, "All he does is send us through the body!" Herman Heart, however, does a lot more than what the blood cells imagine. In order to be a healthy heart, Herman--and all the other hearts out there--has to have a good structure, function properly, and, of course, be loving and romantic.

First Aspect

So what is the key to being a successful, healthy heart? How do all the aspiring hearts in the world start? First, they need a good structure. A healthy heart is usually the size of a clenched fist and might weigh nine ounces for an adult **(Ward 10).** Tom McGowen says that "day and night, day in and day out, whether [we] are standing, sitting, walking, running, awake, or sleeping, a pair of pumps inside [our] body works steadily away, pumping fluid through miles of tiny tubes" **(McGowen 11)**. These pumps that he mentions are the hard-working heart.

To be able to function all day and night, one of the main structures a heart must have is four "chambers" called the ventricles and atria. The atria are the two upper chambers, and the ventricles are the two lower chambers of the heart. A wall dividing the two sides of the heart vertically is called the septum **(Ward 11)**. This is a necessary wall because it separates the oxygenated--or fresh blood--from the deoxygenated--or stale blood **(Ward 11).** In a way, blood is just like water. Water that is polluted and stagnant is harmful, poisoning all that comes in contact with it. Likewise, deoxygenated, stale blood that has been throughout the body can be hazardous. Other parts of the heart that potential hearts need to consider if they want to be healthy, working hearts include the pulmonary arteries, veins and tricuspid, and the semilunar and mitral valves **(McGowen 16).** All in the running for the part of hearts will soon find that their structures and roles are complex but an integral part of life.

Hearts, these days, also need protection from harmful germs and other substances that travel in the bloodstream. To the epicardium, or outside of the heart, the pericardium is the protection **("Heart" n.p.)**. Just like the epidermis protects the corium, the pericardium, a thin bag surrounding the heart, contains a liquid which lubricates and protects the heart.

Obviously Herman Heart's structure in the body is far more complex than the blood cells like to think.

Second Aspect

Now that all the would-be hearts know what type of structure they should have, they need to learn how and why all of the parts of the heart function. To become healthy hearts, they must function properly because if they don't, the whole body is affected. It is kind of like the "I jump; you jump" theory. If the heart has an attack, so does the rest of the body **(Rodale15).** As we already know, the heart has four chambers--two upper and two lower. The left lower ventricle is the strongest of all the chambers because it has one of the most important jobs, which requires the most strength. This particular ventricle has to send blood all the way through the body in one contraction. The right ventricle only has to pump blood to the neighborly lungs, which is much easier **(Ward 11).**

The basic blood circulation route starts at the heart, goes to the lungs, back to the heart, where it is pumped throughout the whole body, and then this cycle repeats itself **(McGowen 12).** During this entire route two different types of blood are going in and out of the heart, oxygenated and deoxygenated blood. The deoxygenated blood comes back from its route and enters the heart through valves and veins and arteries that replenish the CO2 and oxygen that were once in the blood **(Ward 12).**

Some of the major veins and valves, for example, are the superior and inferior venae cavae **("Heart" n.p.).** These are the largest veins in the body, draining blood directly into the heart. The aorta, on the other hand, is the largest artery in the body, receiving blood pumped from the left ventricle **(McGowen).** Hearts must never underestimate the importance of the role of these veins and arteries.

How does a heart beat? The heart doesn't exactly beat in a synchronized manner; it just seems like it. Cardiac muscle is special muscle in the walls of the heart, its contractions causing the heart to pump. Cardiac muscle "consists of threads or muscle fibers, which contract to produce movement. It is very unusual, though, that these fibers are connected in a dense network" **(Ward 14).** This dense network of fibers makes it so that one fiber can contract and spread to the others, which also contract. Even though the fibers contract at different times, the "chemical changes" spread so quickly that it feels and looks like one whole beat **(McGowen 14).**

It is beginning to look as if Herman might be promoted to CEO of the body with all of the power he holds in terms of the functions he manages every minute of every hour of every day.

Third Aspect

Now that all the hearts out there know all the scientific information about structure and function, before their audition they need to learn perhaps the most important process to becoming a mature heart--feelings.

A heart has to love and be romantic. Of course, love is in the headlines of newspapers and the topic of magazine articles. It's what makes romantic movies romantic, and it's what puts the romance in romance novels. It sends people running to the altar, where the lack of it propels them to divorce court. Love truly is "always in the air." As the saying goes, "Love has toppled kings, inspired poets, sparked wars, soothed beasts, and changed the course of history" **("Can't Do...Love" 58).** To aspiring hearts, what does this mean?

"The heart's rhythms are exquisitely tuned to love" **("Can't Do...Love" 59)**; therefore, whatever the heart does affects the way people feel, which in turn affects the way they act. In being a heart, one of the most important steps is learning to love. All around us is evidence of what can happen to people when their hearts don't cooperate.

Cruella Devil's heart, Spike, is a good example of a heart gone awry. He was hard and rough, didn't get along with his blood cells, and refused to replenish blood. How did this affect Cruella? She was hateful and angry her whole life--to the point of almost skinning 101 Dalmatians.

Most hearts, though, have all the necessary romantic parts. One part is the "Golden Rule Chamber," which is filled with love for others and is very fair and equal about whom it loves.

The second chamber is the "Eros Love Chamber." Eros love is the love that we have for something such as music, books, or anything aesthetic that is temporary. **("Can't Do....Love" 60).**

The third chamber that hearts must have is the "Agape Love Chamber." Agape love is the love that is totally opposite of Eros love, as agape love is permanent love that we have for mothers and fathers and other relatives. This chamber goes to work whenever we know love to be lasting.

Finally, the fourth chamber is the "Soul Mate Chamber." This chamber doesn't actually begin working until we finally meet that one person that we're meant to stay with for the rest of our lives.

Looks like there's more to Herman than we thought. Guess he's not "all work and no play" after all. There's a soft, warm spot to him that all hearts must cultivate if they are truly to perform all their duties.

Conclusion

Herman Heart still continues to obediently pump blood through his body. He is still friends with the veins and occasionally talks to the nearby lungs. The blood cells respect Herman now and admire the hard, nonstop work that he does. They finally realize that he--and any competition Herman might have--has to have good structure, function properly, and be loving and romantic every hour of the day.

Ashley Gaudet
How-To Research Paper

How to Be a Perfect 1950's Housewife

Introduction

The year is 1999. The millennium is rapidly approaching. We have CEO's and MBA's and PH.D.'s. We would think that modern times mean modern terms, but who has not--in these "modern times"--referred to women as "housewives"? It's the nineties, and women are still the "chore-doers"! Many present-day women are doctors, lawyers, and nuclear physicists, and the word "housewife" is not part of their vocabulary. However, let's take a trip down memory lane to examine just what their predecessors did to make them earn the title "housewives." What we need to do, then, is to think back to a time when life seemed perfect, when smooth, crystal-clear waters lapped up on white, sandy beaches. We need to think back to the 1950's and what "housewife" meant in that era, namely a "woman, especially a married woman, who manages the home for her family" (Webster's 376). Manage a home for her family? What does it all mean? [Let's travel back and learn how to be that perfect 1950's housewife **by managing the home and kids**, **knowing how to be in style and to fit in,** and **being aware of current events.]**

First Aspect

What woman doesn't get sick of her family sometime--whether it's in the 2000's, 1990's, or 1950's? **However, to manage the home and kids, many believe that a positive attitude is the key.** As the saying goes, "In Heaven an angel is nobody in particular" (Shaw n.p.), so the earthly angel might as well be the 1950's housewife who serves an easy, crunchy breakfast of the new Sugar Pops, just introduced by Kellogg ("Cereal" n.p.), waiting for her kids and husband with a warm "good-morning" smile taped on her face. After all, "there is no love sincerer than the love of food" (Shaw n.p.). The first step, it would seem, for the perfect wife must be to set the family morning to rights and put her loved ones off with clear heads.

While husbands are off at work and kids sent merrily to school, housewives of the 50's start the evening preparations. They clean the house till it shines. They polish and vacuum and wash and spray, and if their hubbies earn a large enough income, they have the privilege of meticulously dusting their painting by the French sculptor/artist Henri Matisse (Lindop 82) and admiring their Eames furniture and wishing they would be given another $4,000 to buy another Charles Eames side chair at Herman Miller's down the road ("Furniture" n.p.). After all, their husbands would be so proud that their little women remember that this is a revolutionary chair made of contour-molded plywood on a frame of aluminum tubing, a chair that won top price a few years earlier in a Museum of Modern Art Organic

Design Competition ("Furniture" n.p.). Just think, the perfect wife can do maid service and be a storehouse of information as well.

With the day spent anticipating the family's arrival, the 50's housewife now has to set herself into high gear when the kids get home from school. There is homework to be done with Mommy's help, baths to be taken with Mommy scrubbing and rub-a-dub-dubbing, and nighttime stories to be read with Mommy using her many voices. While these women are picking up the last few things to ensure that their husbands' arrivals are stress-free, calamities might happen. A ceramic vase, broken earlier in the day, is swept away with no tell-tale signs because "between lovers a confession is a dangerous thing" (Rowland n.p.). To ease their guilt, perhaps many 50's women put on a new, easy-moving record of Frank Sinatra--the best voice out, many say--and like Bing Crosby pronounced, "the voice of a lifetime--but why did it have to be (ours)" ("Bing Crosby" n.p.). The 1950's wife always appreciates a good joke, just as she always makes sure that her husband's Connie Mack-signed baseball (Lindop 88) is still in its place, dust-free, and that their new black-and-white television set with a 19-inch screen, retailing at $187, (Lindop 88) is untouched, no fingerprints and no smudges. A man's home is his castle, after all.

The evening underway, the 1950's woman finishes up the dinner she's been slaving over all day. How proud she is that it contains her man's favorites, but she has decided to lay off the meat after the British beef shortage, which lead to the consumption of horse hocks instead of beef ("1950 food" n.p.). Besides, she thinks, "man is an intelligence, not served by, but in servitude to his organs" (Rowland n.p.), and her number-one priority must be her husband's organs.

Besides the actual meal, the perfect 1950's wife realizes the importance of the perfect ambience. She lights two tall white candles and sets them on the polished dining room table, along with the perfectly prepared food.

The 1950's housewife waits patiently for her husband's arrival and is glad that she can manage the home and kids, and still--somehow--show her love to him. In the back of her perfect mind, though, she recalls the saying that "love (is) the quest; marriage (is) the conquest, and divorce (is) the inquest" (Rowland n.p.). But she decides not to spoil their evening with imperfect thoughts.

Second Aspect

Besides managing the home and kids, the 1950's housewife has to know how to be in style and to fit in. Her husband has already allowed her to purchase her Anne Fogarty dresses--with their narrow waists and wide, frilly skirts--and she has ironed them and neatly hung them in her closet. She realizes that fashion is important in the fifties and that no longer do women wear clothes that reflect the wartime severity and scarcity of material (Lindop 20). However, the middle-class wives still dress like their mothers, wearing hats, gloves, and pearls at every conceivable occasion (Tames 56).

Not only does the 1950's housewife have to worry about her own appearance, she thinks about that of her teenage son, who dresses in blue jeans, checked shirts, sloppy sweaters, and suede shoes (Tames 55). His sister wears clothes with rounded shoulders, tight waists, slightly padded hips, and skirts that are mid-calf or below. And, as all fashion-conscious women know, short hair is very popular--even in pink--as the zany year of 1955 reflected (Lindop 80-81). As for the younger tykes, the 1950's housewife couldn't be prouder to watch them running around wearing Davy Crockett hats and twirling hula-hoops, and--like everyone else--claiming that they saw flying saucers, or just playing the increasingly popular family game, Scrabble (Lindop 81).

But the apple of the 1950's mother's eye is her college boy, who was recently part of setting a national record, the boys at his college claiming they crammed thirty-two people into a phone booth. Some say it was unfair since the booth was lying on the ground, but his 1950's mother couldn't help but be proud of him. After all,

"It's all the young can do for the old, to shock them, and keep them up-to-date" (Shaw n.p.).

And if an adult friend stops by, the *1950's* wife could offer him an *L+M* cigarette--with its "alpha-cellulose" filter tips--which has just been recently introduced by *Liggett* and *Myers* and advertised as "just what the doctor ordered" ("Cigarettes" n.p.). It's not the fault of the *1950's* wife--after all, she's just trying to fit in--that she won't know about the dangers of cigarettes until "cancer by the carton" is published by Reader's Digest ("Cigarettes" n.p.).

So the *1950's* housewife should always be up-to-date with style and know how to fit in. After all, if it will make her husband and kids happy, her mission on Earth will be accomplished.

Third Aspect

How could there be more than managing the house and kids and fitting in? **Besides these two steps, the 1950's wife should always be aware of current events.** She may hate keeping up with politics, and her opinion may be that "if all economists were laid end to end they would not reach a conclusion" (Shaw n.p.), but she'll try for her husband's sake.

Now that CBS has started color network presentations (Lindop 72), she can watch news while he's at work and then discuss it with him when he gets home. She might also talk about how she wishes they could take the kids to Disneyland, recently opened in Anaheim ("Disneyland" n.p.), but if they can't do that, then maybe they could snag a couple of tickets to Under Milkwood or My Fair Lady, which are making big hits in New York.

The perfect 1950's wife could surprise her husband by discussing how there haven't been any leads in the stolen "Stone of Scone" case and how she wishes her family could have gone to the 1953 Olympic games in Finland, but the kids were too little then. She could also show off her current events knowledge in a conversation about how Albert Einstein died, Grace Kelly became a princess, and the great Martin Luther King is leading a fight against prejudice (Sharman 6-7). If that's not enough to impress her better half, she could express her desire to purchase E.B. White's new book <u>Charlotte's Web</u> for their little treasures.

The perfect 1950's housewife can do it all--keeping up with current events hasn't been as hard as she has imagined, especially when the rewards are a satisfied husband.

Conclusion

Now that we realize the steps to becoming perfect 1950's housewives, let's straighten our pearls, fluff our frilly Anne Fogarty dresses, comb our shoulder-length hair, and turn up our Frank Sinatra records to show our husbands what we're made of. They're so proud they haven't even missed the broken vases. **We have easily achieved our goals by following three simple approaches: managing the house and family, knowing how to be in style and fit in, and being up-to-date on current events.**

Name:____________________ Class:________________ Date:____________

How-To Research Rubric #1
Documentation

1. To prove that you have **blended your quoted material** with your own words, list a **blended quote** from your paper and the appropriate **footnote.**

   ☞ Remember to watch for creating **run-ons** when blending your words with those from a text.

____

____

____

2. Besides documenting quoted material, attribution must be given for **paraphrased ideas** as well. Give an example from your paper of a paraphrased idea, complete with its **footnote.**

____

____

____

3. Some footnotes are not simply the author's last name and page number. Give an example of one of your **footnotes that varies from this format.**

____

____

Name:____________________ Class:________________ Date:__________

How-To Research Rubric #2
STRUCTURE

Using your **rough draft**, answer the following questions, **revising your draft** as necessary.

I. Introduction

A. Explain what **method** you used to **introduce your topic** (e.g., series of questions, short narrative scenario, quotations, etc.) and how you feel it is effective:

1. Method:____________________

2. Effect:____________________

____

B. List the **three aspects in your thesis statement** and explain how they are **parallel** (e.g., all verbs, all nouns, etc.):

1. ASPECTS:

a.____________________

b.____________________

c.____________________

2. PARALLEL STRUCTURE: ____________________

II. Body paragraphs

A. List the **three main steps** (three "aspects") in your body paragraphs and their **subpoints.**

1. **STEP #ONE:** ______________________________
   a. ______________________________
   b. ______________________________
   c. ______________________________

2. **STEP #TWO:** ______________________________
   a. ______________________________
   b. ______________________________
   c. ______________________________

3. **STEP #THREE:** ______________________________
   a. ______________________________
   b. ______________________________
   c. ______________________________

B. List how many **paragraphs** you have for each aspect and explain **why you changed paragraphs** within an aspect.

1. **Aspect #one:** ______________________________

   Reason: ______________________________

2. **Aspect #two:** ______________________________

   Reason: ______________________________

3. **Aspect #three:** ______________________________

Reason:______________________________________

III. Conclusion

A. Explain what **method** you used to conclude your paper and how it is **effective**:

1. **METHOD:**______________________________________

2. **EFFECT:**______________________________________

B. Did you remember to **restate your thesis and three points**?_______________________

Name:______________________________**Class:**______________**Date:**____________

How-To Research Rubric #3
Revising/Proofreading

1. Sentence Structure Variety--To prove that you have included VARIOUS TYPES OF SENTENCES in your paper, list an example of each of the following:

A. SIMPLE SENTENCE:____

____

B. COMPOUND SENTENCE: ____

____

C. COMPLEX SENTENCE:____

____

D. INVERTED ORDER:____

____

E. NOUN ABSOLUTE:____

____

F. PARTICIPIAL PHRASE:____

____

2. Sentence Structure Revision--To prove that you have attempted "DEEP REVISION," give two examples of sentences "BEFORE" and "AFTER" revisions.

A.

1. BEFORE:____

____

2. AFTER:____

____

B.

1. BEFORE:____

____

2. AFTER:____

____

3. Mechanical Errors-- To prove that you have checked for mechanical errors, list three examples of proofreading that you have done, using three different types of errors (E.G., RUN-ONS, FRAGMENTS, SPELLING, SUBJECT/VERB AGREEMENT, ETC.)

A.____

B.____

C.____

Name:____________________ Class:____________ Date:____________

Final Check Sheet for How-To Research Paper

Papers are to be in this order:

1. **Cover Sheet** (Title in middle; heading lower right)

2. **Outline & Final Web**

   A. Your outline will have **five Roman numerals.**

   B. Body paragraphs will have **three subdivisions** listed as "A," "B," and "C" and at least **two subpoints** under each letter, which will be listed as "1" and "2."

   C. All divisions must be **parallel in structure.**

   D. Outline should not be a sentence outline but a **phrase** (topic) **outline.**

3. **Two Final Typed Copies of Research Paper**

   A. Each part of the paper will be typed as **separate parts;** for instance, the first point will not be typed on the same page as the introduction.

   B. **Internal footnotes will be color-coded** to correspond to note cards and bibliographic cards used as support, each source representing a different color. Remember to footnote all facts, not just quoted facts.

   C. **Box in the key word,** the main reason, for each of the three points. Next, put a **check mark on each detail** that supports this point.

D. **Label five READING/literary elements** (e.g., inference, cause/effect, fact/opinion, main idea, detail, figurative language devices, etc.)

4. Three State-Mandated Reading/Literature Questions Relating to Paper

A. Questions must be related to **student's own individual weaknesses** in terms of reading/literature objectives.

B. **Answer choices** should be in the format of four multiple choices.

5. Bibliography/Works Cited

A. Be sure to include only those sources that you actually cited in your paper--**a minimum of five.**

B. Be sure to **alphabetize** your entries and follow the form given.

C. Entries should be **color-coded** to correspond to the footnotes in your paper.

6. Note Cards

A. Note cards will be **color-coded,** put in the order they appear in the paper, stapled to blank typing paper, and placed after the Works Cited.

B. Include all **vocabulary cards**--whether they were used in the paper or not.

7. Rough Copies/Student Response Sheets/Rubrics--

All rough copies/response sheets will be included at the end.

Due Date:____________________________________

Don't forget parent signature on final draft.

How to Use Response Sheet

1. If students present their papers to the class, the class can be instructed to use the "Response Sheet" to take notes on the following aspects of the presentation:

   a. Topic
   b. Three main steps involved in "how-to" process
   c. An interesting fact
   d. Three Smiley-Face devices (See "Smiley-Face Tricks")
   e. Problems the class observed
   f. Answers to student author's questions regarding aspects of his/her paper (Student author might want to write on the board questions for the class to consider while the paper is being presented.)

2. The teacher can call on students to orally answer various questions from the "Response Sheet," giving students oral response grades for being "active participants."

3. Students may play Musical Chairs, going to only four or five classmates' desks, answering the "Response Sheet" questions.

4. The "Response Sheet" can be used as a "rubric" during the rough draft stage to provide feedback to the student author before the final draft.

Name:______________________ Class:________________ Date:__________

Response Sheet
How-To Research Papers

Writer:______________________

1. Topic:______________________
2. Three steps:____________, ________________, ________________
3. Interesting fact:______________________________________
4. Three smiley-face parts:____________________________________,
   ____________________________,& ______________________________
5. Problems:____
   ____
6. Answers to Student Questions:__________, ____________, __________

Writer:______________________

1. Topic:______________________
2. Three steps:____________, ____________, __________________
3. Interesting fact:______________________________________
4. Three smiley-face parts:____________________________________,
   ____________________________,& ______________________________
5. Problems:____
   ____
6. Answers to Student Questions:__________, ____________, ________

PART VII

INTERNET RESEARCH

Using Internet Activities

Plan Your Perfect Vacation

1. "Plan Your Perfect Vacation" provides students with practice in taking note cards, summarizing information, quoting when applicable, and citing sources.

2. The information can be used to write a **descriptive paper**, where students describe the "perfect" accommodations, sights, activities, and various other features to be considered in planning a trip.

3. Or the paper could be a **persuasive paper**, arguing that the chosen vacation is indeed the "perfect" one.

4. A **narrative** could be required by weaving information into a story. Virtually **any mode** could be the end result.

5. Or the assignment could be **shared in class**--without the student writing a paper--by having **informal "talks"** regarding the researched findings.

What a Fun Time!

1. Not only do students have **fun** with this assignment, but they become more acquainted with local cities on-line events/activities, restaurants, and shopping networks.

2. Again, a **paper could result**, or the **gathering of the information** could be the end product itself.

Poetry Connection

1. **"Poetry Connection"** works well with a **comparison/contrast writing unit** in that it requires students to locate a poem that in some way relates to their library book or in-class novel.

2. Students must peruse various books of poetry, locate the poem, and explain the connection in a 250-word essay.

3. Also, the assignment reinforces the study of figurative language, weaving quoted material with the student writer's own words, and citing sources.

Allusions! Get the Message?

1. **"Allusions! Get the Message?"** helps emphasize the importance of students understanding allusions in a literary work.

2. Although this particular assignment is for the novel **Thwonk**, students can still be asked to **explain the allusions**, thus getting practice in locating the source of allusions and becoming more aware of allusions themselves.

3. Teachers can use this assignment as a **model** in making a similar sheet for a work studied in class. When students are asked to explain not only the allusion but how the allusion adds to the story, their level of understanding of the literary work is greatly enhanced.

This Reminds Me...

1. **"This Reminds Me..."** gives students practice in determining rising actions, climax, and falling action(s) of a novel.

2. Students must **quote the events**, giving an internal footnote, and explaining how each event is representative of actions taking place in the work.

3. Students are then required to use the **Internet** to locate a FAMOUS QUOTATION that relates to the quoted actions of their library books.

4. Again, students must **explain the connection**.

Name: ______________________ **Class:** ____________ **Date:** ____________

Plan Your Perfect Vacation

Using the **Internet and CD-ROM**, plan the **ideal vacation.** Be sure to **cite your sources** in the proper form and **summarize** the information in your own words, unless--for a certain reason--you need to quote a passage.

1. **Brainstorm five places** you would choose to visit if you could go anywhere in the world.

A. ______________________ B. ______________________ C. ______________________

D. ______________________ E. ______________________

Choose three of the above places to research.

2. Look up the "perfect" **accommodations** and take three note cards for each.

Note Card #1

Note Card #2

Note Card #3

Bibliographic Card

Staple any extra bibliographic cards on back of worksheet.

3. Now research information regarding **three famous sights.**

Note Card #1

Note Card #2

Note Card #3

Bibliographic Card

4. Cite one **activity** (THREE NOTE CARDS) that you would enjoy.

Note Card #1

Note Card #2

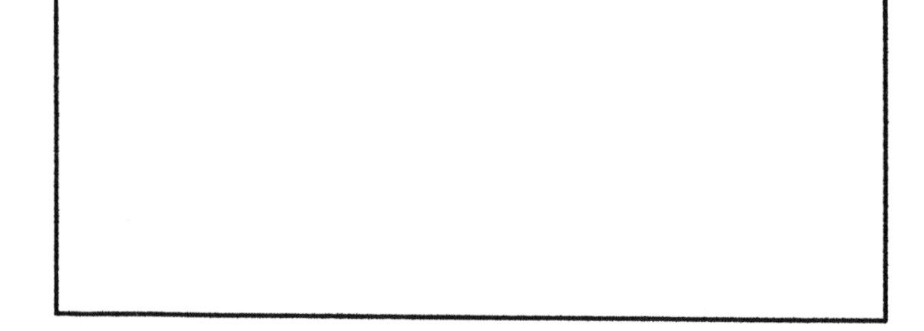

Note Card #3

Bibliographic Card

5. **Choose two other aspects** (e.g., money exchange rate, climate, language, etc.) **about which you feel you need information. Write two note cards and appropriate bibliographic cards.**

Note Card #1

Note Card #2

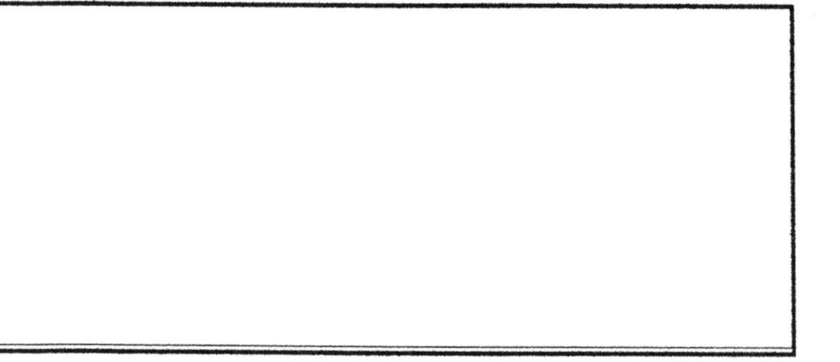

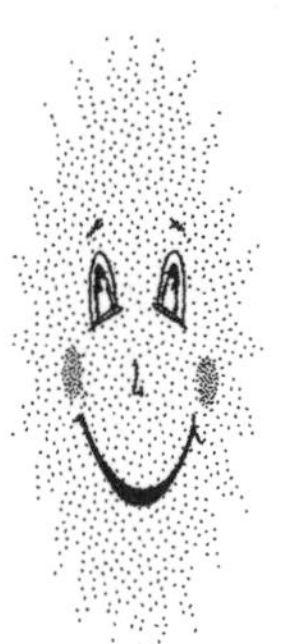

Bibliographic Card

Name:______________________________ Class:______________ Date:______________

What a Fun Time!

Using the **Internet,** create the **perfect date** that could occur within a 60-**mile radius of your hometown.** Be sure to take the appropriate note and bibliographic cards.

1. You and your date can go to any **restaurant** within the area. For once, money is no object. Using the Web Site, locate two **restaurants** that you (and your date) would enjoy and take two **note cards apiece,** plus the appropriate **bibliographic cards.**

2. After your dinner out, you and your date will go to an **activity** of your choice. Choose two **possible ideas for entertainment,** take **two note cards apiece,** and the **bibliographic cards** to go with them.

3. Since this evening you don't have to worry about money, choose **two gift ideas** to give your date as a present for the evening. Take **two note cards** for each and **bibliographic cards.**

Name:____________________ Class:______________ Date:________________

Poetry Connection

Assignment:

1. In the library peruse several **poetry books** and choose one that might have a poem that is in some way **connected to your current novel**:____.

2. In **considering the connections**, think of the following:

   a. Theme(s)
   b. Characters--remember the six aspects of characterization
   c. Conflict--internal and/or external
   d. Central tone/mood

   ✏ The idea is to select a **central or major theme, etc.** as opposed to an **obscure** one.

3. Once you have found a poem that "**fits**" **an important concept** in your novel, do the following:

   a. Type the poem, paying attention to line divisions, punctuation, etc.
   b. Write a bibliographic entry for the book.
   c. Explicate the poem in terms of any figurative language devices.
   d. In at least 250 typed words, explain the connection to your novel, using at least three quotes from the novel and two from the poem.

   ✏ Be sure to use your **literary analysis skills**: blending quotes--remembering the special method of quoting poetry--adding persuasive explanations, and including internal footnotes.

Name:______________________Class:________________Date:__________________

Allusions! Get the Message?

The following are examples of **allusions** from **Thwonk** by Joan Bauer. To fully understand the text, readers need to be aware of **meaningful references**. For the following, **explain the allusion** and give an explanation of **how the allusion adds to the story.**

1. Stieglitz (5)

   a. Explanation:____

   ____

   b. Effect on story:____

   ____

2. Oracle (26)

   a. ____

   ____

   b. ____

   ____

3. Ansel Adams (63)

   a. ____

   ____

b.

4. Raphael fresco (81)

a.

b.

5. Ruben's "Head of a Child"

a.

b.

6. Sistine Chapel (103)

a.

b.

7. King Solomon (104)

Allusions

a.

b.

8. Cliff Notes (107)

a.

b.

9. Inner Sanctum (116)

a.

b.

10. Peace Corps (139)

a.

b.

____

11. A Streetcar Named Desire (143)

    a. ______________________________

    ____

    b. ______________________________

    ____

12. Jonathan Livingston Cupid (149)

    a. ______________________________

    ____

    b. ______________________________

    ____

13. Alice in Wonderland (152)

    a. ______________________________

    ____

    b. ______________________________

    ____

Allusions

14. Sleeping Beauty (152)

a. ______________________________

____

b. ______________________________

____

15. "Dragnet" (154)

a. ______________________________

____

b. ______________________________

____

16. Henry Higgins/Eliza Doolittle (160)

a. ______________________________

____

b. ______________________________

____

17. Emperor's New Clothes (177)

a. ______________________________

____

b. ______________________________

____

18. "I think that I shall never say
A name as lovely as A.J." (180)

a. ______________________________

____

b. ______________________________

____

19. BLACK HOLE (210)

a. ______________________________

____

b. ______________________________

____

20. Inner child (213)

a. ______________________________

____

b. ______________________________

____

Name:__________________________Class:______________Date:______________

This Reminds Me...

I. Using your **library book**, do the following:

A. Quote what you consider to be the **three most important rising actions**, the **climax**, and a significant **falling action**. Be sure to include an **internal footnote** (author's last name and page number) and a **bibliographic entry** for the book.

B. In your own words, **explain in detail** what is happening in terms of the **plot** at each of these points. In essence, all of your explanations will amount to a **summary** of the book, as you will tell the beginning, middle, and end. Remember when writing about literature to use the **present tense**.

II. Using the **Internet, CDROM, or a quotation book**, do the following:

A. Cite a **quotation** that represents in some way the library book's quotes. Give a bibliographic entry for each.

B. In your own words, **explain the connection.**

III. **Presenting and grading** your project:

A. Your project must be **typed** and displayed in a **creative, visual manner** (e.g., a symbol that represents your book, a plot graph, etc.). Each point of plot must be accompanied by a **picture** (graphic, hand-drawn, magazine cut-out, etc.).

B. You will be graded on the **thoroughness of your explanations** for both the library book and the quotes as well as on **grammatical correctness**.

IV. Example:

A. **Quote from library book:** " 'I'll carry the pails... This once let me haul everything....I want to feel all there is to feel....Let me feel tired....I mustn't forget, I'm alive'" (Bradbury 11).

Bibliographic Entry: Bradbury, Ray. Dandelion Wine. New York: Bantam, 1969.

B. **Explanation:** SINCE DOUGLAS SPAULDING, THE TWELVE-YEAR-OLD PROTAGONIST FROM 1928 GREEN TOWN, ILLINOIS, REALIZES FOR THE FIRST TIME THAT HE IS "ALIVE," HE WANTS TO EXPERIENCE EVERYTHING LIFE HAS TO OFFER. HE ASKS HIS FATHER TO LET HIM "CARRY THE PAILS" OF BERRIES AS A SYMBOL THAT HE IS BECOMING CAPABLE OF DOING A "MAN'S" JOB. IN THIS RITE OF PASSAGE SECTION, DOUGLAS ALSO REALIZES THAT LIFE--GROWTH--CAN BE "TIRING," THAT BECOMING A MAN CAN INDEED BE HARD.

C. **Quote from quotation book:** **"Growth is the only evidence of life" (Newman 490).**

Bibliographic Entry: Bartlett, John, ed. Bartlett's Familiar Quotations. Boston: Little, Brown, & Co., 1982.

D. **Explanation of Connection:** Douglas realizes that "growth is the only evidence of life" and actually wants to record this "growth" in his journal under "Discoveries and Revelations." Douglas's "thinking about it, noticing it," emphasizes that he knows a change is taking place within him, like "finding out maybe that Grandpa or Dad don't (sic) know everything in the world" (Bradbury 19).

WRITING RESEARCH PROJECTS *Activities Kit*

Ready-to-Use Lessons & Activities to Build Research & Writing Skills for Grades 7-12

MARY ELLEN LEDBETTER

This unique resource gives secondary English teachers a refreshing new approach to research-based writing that takes students step-by-step through the process of writing research papers in all modes, provides dozens of award-winning student and teacher models, and offers a variety of in-class projects that can be done on a biweekly basis.

Included are scores of reproducible assignments that introduce students to the various aspects of research and involve them in writing six different types of research papers. Specially designed teacher pages throughout give instructions, suggestions and variations, and built-in student syllabuses, rubrics and tests foster independent work.

For easy use, the *Kit* is printed in a big 8 1/4" x 11" spiral-bound format that folds flat for photocopying of all student materials and is organized into seven parts:

- **LIBRARY PROJECTS** includes a variety of classroom assignments to familiarize students with the elements of research, such as documenting facts taken from text *(Dear Diary)*, incorporating quoted textual material into their own words *(Letter to the Author)*, and writing note and bibliographic cards.
- **NARRATIVE RESEARCH** provides models such as Maureen Daly's *Sixteen* for analyzing literary elements and researched facts, and syllabuses *(Narrative Research Syllabuses; Two Variations)*, rubrics *(Rubric #1: Research Narrative Vignette)*, and final check sheets to guide students in writing their own research narratives.
- **PERSUASIVE RESEARCH** activities give students the opportunity to role play *(You Are the Author)*, to experiment with persuasion in another genre *(Library Book Test-Poem Form)*, and to experience the unique concept of using narrative scenario introductions and conclusions as attention-getters for more traditional persuasive research papers.
- **COMPARISON/CONTRAST RESEARCH** includes projects that give students practice in being artist and writer in a library book test *(Illustrator and Author)*, writing classificatory papers elaborated by researched facts, and revising their comparison/contrast research papers according to student-interactive rubrics.
- **DESCRIPTIVE RESEARCH** presents a *Methods of Elaboration* rubric and examples to help students learn various ways to provide detail/support within an essay and a *Library Book Test/Descriptive Mode* assignment that reinforces all stages of the writing process as students describe three memorable scenes from their book.
- **HOW-TO (PROCESS) RESEARCH** focuses on writing from someone else's point of view *(You Are the Teacher)* and includes sample research papers across the curriculum, in science ("How to Be a Heart"), history ("How to Be a Perfect 1950's Housewife"), and language arts ("The Business of Writing").
- **INTERNET RESEARCH** features projects that demonstrate Internet capabilities for doing research. In *Plan Your Perfect Vacation*, students take notes on accommodations, sights, money exchange and other aspects of vacationing. In *This Reminds Me...*, they find quotations that complement the rising actions, climax, and denouement of a library book.

In short, **WRITING RESEARCH PROJECTS ACTIVITIES KIT** offers a stimulating and practical new way to give your students the guidelines, models, and assignments they need to develop their research and writing skills and learn how to apply these skills to the different kinds of research writing.

About the Author

Mary Ellen Ledbetter (B.A., English, speech, Western Michigan University; M.A., Engl Michigan State University) has taught in public schools in Michigan and Texas and at San College in Pasadena, Texas. She received Goose Creek CISD's Board of Trustees' Bell A Outstanding Teacher in 1995 and 1997 and is currently a presenter/consultant for the Bu Education and Research in Bellevue, Washington. Her resource, *Writing Portfolio Activiti* was published by the Center in 1998.

2281F-3

ISBN 0-13-022816-8

90000

9 780130 228161

THE CENTER FOR APPLIED RESEARCH IN EDUCATION
West Nyack, NY 10994

www.PHedu.com

Cover Design by Juan S. DeGuzman